Let's Get Comfortable

How to furnish and decorate a welcoming home

Meredith® Books
Des Moines, Iowa

Let's Get Comfortable
How to furnish and decorate a welcoming home

Mitchell Gold and Bob Williams

with Mindy Drucker

Principal Photographers: Sally Fanjoy and James Labrenz

Meredith Books
1716 Locust Street
Des Moines, Iowa 50309-3023
meredithbooks.com

Printed in China

First Edition
Library of Congress Control Number: 2006930043
ISBN: 978-0-696-23430-9

Book Design by Doug Turshen with David Huang

In memory of Bob's sister, Melissa Williams,
and father, Hank Bauerlein.
Their caring spirits live on. —M.G + B.W.

To Mitchell's brother, Richard, always our biggest
fan and source of support. —B.W. + M.G.

To Rhoda and Jack Gold, who loved what Mitchell and
I were doing from the beginning and who raised a son
with an extraordinarily generous spirit. — B.W.

To Carolyn Bauerlein, who wouldn't accept her son
being anything less than all he could be and who
raised him to be a real "gentle-man." —M.G.

contents

93

148

03

68

130

DAIRY AND POULTRY
FEEDS
T LEAST ... PRODUCE MORE

12

206

123

151

142

Take It From Lulu: How To Use This Book

What does a bulldog know about decorating? Plenty. Just like all good dogs, Lulu, our English bulldog and company mascot, knows that comfort comes first. In fact, we're sure she would say the whole point of decorating is to create a welcoming home for you, your family, your guests, and, of course, your pets. Along with Lulu, we're here to help you do that with style.

Although we hail from two pretty different places—Trenton, New Jersey for Mitchell, and Dallas, Texas for Bob—we've always had a love of comfort in common. This synergy has led us not only to create a furniture company dedicated to that principle but also to develop a relaxed style of designing and decorating homes. What we've learned along the way, you'll find in this book.

Our book provides both visual inspiration and practical advice. Part I shows how our homes and the homes of some comfort-minded friends are decorated and furnished. Part II offers "Comfort Lessons" to help you create an at-home feeling in either specific styles, such as country and modern, or in a mix of several styles. You'll also learn to:

> **" Here's what worries me: As '50s design sees a resurgence, will I start liking those ugly clown paintings again? Or worse, that batik shirt?"**
> *—Mitchell in the Golds' 1950s den in New Jersey*

- Reduce "fear of furnishing" by thinking of it as collecting rather than decorating
- Arrange furniture and accessories to create rooms that are easy to live in
- Make furniture selection the heart of your decorating process
- Expand your ideas of which furniture options are available

Our book also takes into account that you may not have as much time as you'd like to devote to furnishing your home—or have a decorator on call. Most of the furnishings are easily accessible, and the arrangements are manageable to reproduce. The book is not a catalog, but, of course, it mainly uses our furniture. If you like our style sense and enjoy living as comfortably as we do, you easily can find items like these to help you create these looks in our stores and in specialty home stores around the country. Rather than high-end antiques, these

❝ When you're growing up, you never know what will influence you. Meet the original slipcovered sofa in my life."
–*Bob at home in Texas with Daisy, 1967*

are affordable furnishings—made even more so by our advice on how rooms can be assembled over time rather than all at once and how pieces you own can be used in a new mix.

Finally, to make the settings in this book truly your own, you need only personalize them with favorite collectibles and family photos. You need not be obsessed to have great fun doing this. Visiting flea markets, antiques stores, and art galleries wherever we travel has enriched our homes and our lives. We highly recommend you try it and hope our tips will lead to your own memorable finds.

To us, comfort always will mean more than the "sit" of a sofa or the well-worn patina of wood. It includes the way a room looks: whether it feels balanced, uses soothing colors, is convenient for entertaining, and contains special pieces that reflect your personality. It also includes the experience of shopping for furnishings. And it involves intangibles, such as the gracious way you treat guests in your home and those whose lives you touch daily.

Part of our love of comfort in all forms comes from knowing what it's like to be uncomfortable…from growing up being bullied and not accepted for who we were. In our case it was for being gay, but we know it is equally painful no matter what excuse people use for discriminating against others. And so along with making life more comfortable through our style sense and our furnishings, we are equally committed to helping eliminate that type of discomfort for everyone.

We are excited to help guide you in your quest for a more welcoming home. Please visit our website, www.mgandbw.com, for more tips and insights into our ever-evolving vision of relaxed living. May your home also continue to evolve so that, through all the phases of your life, its comforts truly suit you.

❝ Something my daddies taught me: Making yourself comfortable is one thing, but knowing how to make others comfortable is a really special thing."
–*Lulu at home in North Carolina, 1997*

PART 1

Furnishing the Comfortable Life

How We Make Ourselves at Home

**" When a home is
successfully furnished,
just walking in the door
is like getting a hug."
—*Mitchell***

CHAPTER 1
Welcome Home
The comfort mix mastered in a relaxing lakeside retreat

In building Camp Hickory, Mitchell's house near our North Carolina furniture factory, we learned that comfort is many things: It's the way a room looks—a balance of color and form that's soothing to the eye. It's the way the furniture sits. It's how convenient the space is for entertaining. And it's how personally connected we are to the room through the special things we put on display.

COMFORT COMES NATURALLY. With white trim, cedar shingles, a front porch, and picket fence, Camp Hickory, Mitchell's lakeside North Carolina home, is inviting from first approach, opposite. At the back of the house, windows and decks offer tranquil water views through the pines, this page. The gazebo by the dock is a favorite spot for relaxing at sunset.

" When people walk into Camp Hickory, they say, 'I feel so at home here.' That's our mission: to create spaces where everyone—family, friends, guests, and pets—feels welcome." —*Mitchell*

When it comes to comfort, dogs are naturals. For our English bulldog, Lulu, it's as simple as sunshine through an open window, warming the chair she chose for snoozing. As Lulu would say if she could, "It ain't that complicated." So we've made "simple" our mantra. At Camp Hickory that means neutral textured walls, natural flooring, and simple window treatments as a tranquil background to great views and a rich mix of furnishings. The house is new construction, designed to look old. "We started with the 1920s but wanted more than a certain time period," Bob says. "We envisioned a place where generations of a family could have lived, one that had been expanded and opened up—a fishing cabin that had evolved into a home. That's why there are so many pieces from different eras; it's as if they've been added over the last 80 years." The result, personalized with family photos and favorite collections, is warm, relaxed, and inviting. ⟫ Room by room, here's how we made a comfortable home in the country.

BULLISH ABOUT BULLDOGS. We began collecting bulldogs when Lulu was a pup. As her fame grew, through appearances in our ads and even on a magazine cover, we started getting bulldogs as gifts—in abundance. This has its advantages: Items make a bigger impact grouped, as is evident on the shelves of the rustic hutch. With such a big collection, however, we always have to edit—and hope guests understand if their gift isn't among the current display. Shelves provide opportunities to refresh and rearrange.

Balance is key to a relaxed effect. It starts with the architecture. Here, we offset the staircase with a three-section hutch Bob designed in Adirondack style, reflecting our fishing-cabin inspiration for the house. We chose the hutch over a fireplace because it has unique character and saved money we could use elsewhere. With abundant display and storage, including a TV in the center cabinet, the hutch is also more practical than a fireplace, which often doesn't get used as planned.

UNIQUE BUT NOT ANTIQUE: Accentuating the room's height is a large round iron chandelier from an L.A. junk shop. Bob spotted it hanging 20 feet in the air, painted gold, with all of its candleholders bent. We had it rewired at a lighting store—a surprisingly affordable process that makes buying old lights practical—then sandblasted it and painted it matte black. Accessory-wise, no one item at Camp Hickory is particularly rare or costly. Most are from flea markets, junk stores, or attics, but they seem valuable because they are part of collections.

WARM GLOW. Windows overlooking the lake brighten the double-height living room, opposite. We found all but one of the group portraits, above left, at flea markets, disciplining ourselves to spending less than $50 on each. The bottom photograph, however, is priceless: It's Mitchell's dad's Army battalion, a gift from Mitchell's brother, Richard. The photos generate warmth and interest. And besides, who can resist a man in uniform?

COLOR STORY: The striped rug inspired the butter, raisin, and chalky-blue scheme. We used mainly solid fabrics and included each hue at least twice to help blend the mix of furniture styles. **TWO IN ONE:** Entertaining is a regular event here. The room can seat a dozen yet is uncluttered enough to allow standing room. To prevent loneliness after the crowd leaves, there are two cozy groupings—an armless "sofette" with slipper chairs and a roll-arm sofa with club chair. The rug links the two groups.

NO FUSS. The mix of furnishings helps create the relaxed mood, opposite. Alone, some pieces might be formal, but in combination they feel fresh and original. The prewashed cottons, faux suedes, and vintage leathers are soft to the touch and easy to maintain. Wood is distressed, allaying fears about making the first nick. Simple draperies, above, are all that's needed to frame the view. Across from the "sofette," a slipcovered roll-arm sofa, right, is ideal for reclining. To enliven the wall behind it, we hung a favorite painting from our collection of outsider art, *Yellow Cab* by Laura Craig McNellis. Outsider art is a term used to describe work by self-taught artists uninfluenced by the mainstream art world. Often, they are gifted creators with developmental disabilities. Laura, a talented painter who is autistic, creates art, humorous and moving in its simplicity, that seems like a visual diary of her day.

"A mirror, especially an antiqued one, can be another piece of art in your arrangement. As you move around the room, the 'picture' changes, depending on what's being reflected."—*Bob*

Suit a formal dining room to the country by choosing simple but richly finished wood pieces with just enough detail to feel dressed up. The Dutch country table and sideboard have artfully turned legs. The sideboard has a chamfered front edge, appealing at eye level when you're seated. Using a sideboard instead of a breakfront also lightens the room. **PLACEMENT SERVICE:** When not in use, the cabriole-leg armchairs sit by the sideboard, allowing wider paths through the room. Slipcovering side chairs in washable white denim softens the look, eases care, and allows for visual change. **BALANCING ACT:** A wall display strengthens the house's generations-old feel. Bob began with a 4-foot-wide Venetian-style mirror with distressing, scored lines, and glass rosettes. He flanked it with two large prints, then added smaller pieces from bottom to top. Note that none of these flea market finds costs more than $20 yet together they make an impact.

EVERY PICTURE TELLS A STORY.
On a console facing the front door, above right, Mitchell's family photos, all in white frames, form a welcoming committee. Switching from a mix of frame styles to uniform white was an affordable option with big impact: It cleaned up the view into the living room. Bob used a similar unifying technique in the dining room, opposite. Frames are close in width and tone, giving the pictures similar visual weight.

" A dining porch combines two pleasures: sitting and eating. This is a table we enjoy spending time at." —Bob

Originally an extra place to seat guests at big dinner parties, this porch off the main dining area quickly became a favorite eating spot. At first it was only screened in, but then we added casement windows to allow use year-round. Bob painted the wicker chairs pale green to complement the outdoors. Perfect for a porch, the chairs offer textural contrast to the wood farm table. The room feels cozy because the table and chairs fill the space. Two folk art stools topped with lush ferns add a sense of symmetry. Note the floor's white stenciled stars: They add pattern to the room without distracting from the scenery.

THE POWER OF GROUPING. See the effect in the bloom-filled bottles, above left and opposite. Elegant and inexpensive, they have an informal feel, are easy to see over, and can be moved aside instead of removed at serving time. You don't need many flowers, so you can splurge on a few special ones. Or with such simple vessels, wildflowers work great too.

" This bedroom casts a spell on Lulu and me every time we enter it." —*Mitchell*

Major mixing went on in this bedroom, yet tranquillity reigns. A platform bed with padded headboard and upholstered base encourages nighttime reading and gives a finished look without a bedskirt. A leather ottoman permits pulling on socks—or napping if you're a bulldog. Unmatched nightstands offer their own special pleasures: A mirrored chest provides storage and reflects light, while a fabulously detailed round wood table adds warmth and softens the room's lines.

SERENITY CENTRAL. In the bedroom, opposite, Bob built in architecture with white paneled wainscoting and balanced it visually by painting the wall above it a soothing blue. We kept the floor informal with simple wood planks and added rustic texture with a sisal rug. Striped pillows are the only pattern. A sense of calm comes from solid colors such as the olive leather on the chair, above. A chest as a nightstand, right, has room on top for a lamp, books, flowers, McCoy pottery, and an outsider art painting whose creator extended his talents to the frame.

> **People often forget about the ceiling. They're focused on walls and floors. But especially in a bedroom, it sure makes sense to consider it."** —*Bob*

The bedroom's "ta-da" element is its coffered ceiling. We gathered pictures of similar ones and worked with a contractor to create our own. While it's no DIY project, a coffered ceiling can be built by a contractor or a handyperson from 1×5s, 2×4s, and moldings. It's a great feature that can be added to a room at any time. To balance the architectural elements of the ceiling and wainscoting, we dressed the windows in formal pinch-pleat linen draperies with valances. Behind the draperies, Roman shades help keep out light for sleeping late. We had the luxury of creating a second seating area: a daybed beside the window, where Mitchell enjoys his morning diet cola. Next to it is one of Bob's lucky flea market finds, a 19th-century basket-weave table with splayed legs that mirror the daybed's flared lines.

BATH TIME. Wood doors from a Paris saloon divide bedroom and bath, right. The bath has lighter-blue walls and white cabinetry that echoes the wainscoting. Mitchell always wanted a bath or dressing room with a round table; he loves the look and convenience. It's good for laying out a rolling bag to pack. (And it's not a valuable antique so humidity is not a concern.) A slipcovered terry cloth stool adds a pleasing touch.

CHAPTER 2
Let Us Entertain You
Public and private pleasures in a modern house in town

A minimum of "stuff" can be very comfortable as long as it's the right stuff. In this '50s ranch that we renovated with large-group entertaining in mind, a soothing and practical mix of furnishings works in tandem with its tranquil shell. The result suits not only our relaxed style of hosting but also those much-too-infrequent quiet evenings at home.

INVITING INSIDE AND OUT. Coming home to this renovated 1950s ranch is the perfect end to the day, whether we're arriving alone or bringing a crowd. On party nights guests pulling into the circular drive get a welcoming view through the kitchen windows of our company chef preparing dinner. The portico is a rainy-weather bonus: Be dropped off and stay dry. The commercial-grade storefront-glass entry is a prelude to the modern interior.

W

e love to entertain, and lucky for us, it's part of our jobs. As founders of a furniture company, we enjoy hosting customers, employees, and the press during home-furnishings trade shows in High Point, North Carolina. For years, we took guests to restaurants but always wanted to treat them to a laid-back evening at home. We also tired of hotels and wanted the comfort of our own stuff. So together we bought a 1950s ranch and renovated it with entertaining in mind. >>> Here's what we learned about making a house relaxing for guests and rejuvenating for its owners when the party's over.

SOPHISTICATED COMFORT FOOD. Guests savor the specialties of MG+BW corporate chef Sean Robinson (middle row, second photo from left), who also runs our furniture factory's health-conscious gourmet cafe. The dining room often serves as a buffet station (top row, center). Eating takes place on the patio (top row, left), in the living room, and in a glass-enclosed sunroom set up with dining tables—as shown in the bottom row, center, with Mitchell toasting guest of honor Tipper Gore.

Making people feel at home begins at the front door. Much more than a pass-through, the entry sets the comfortable tone for your home.

Sophisticated living and entertaining weren't the first things that came to mind when we saw this 3,500-square-foot ranch. Two major changes took it to the next level: letting in light and using the same materials from room to room. **LIGHT'S THE WAY:** With natural illumination, any room is more inviting. Sun flows into the entry through a doorway to the living room, which we brightened by replacing the exterior wall with commercial storefront glass. **SMART IDEA:** While the glass wall was a big budget item, another brightening technique saved money. Instead of ripping out the original dark-brown tongue-and-groove paneling, we painted it a warm white. We also painted ceilings the same white and installed wood flooring. **STORY TO TELL:** For a satisfying addition to an entry, include a unique piece. Bob chose a handcarved Dogon ladder, used by African tribes in Mali to reach their cliffside homes and considered a symbolic link between this world and the next.

LESS IS MORE. Minimally furnished, the entry, opposite, immediately establishes a sense of serenity. Its spare decor also makes accommodating large groups easier. The paneling and floor form a shell against which the furnishings stand out. A wood-framed floor mirror reflects light, serves as a focal point, and allows "one last look" as you head out the door. Beside it, a slender metal table topped with an orchid forms a graceful mid-height shape that helps balance the mirror and the African ladder in the corner. A sisal rug supplies texture, warmth, and protection for the wood floor. Note the convenient coat closet at the ready. On the patio, above left, we ensure that a bath-loving Lulu smells pretty for company.

In the living room, a few beautiful pieces create a comfortable seating area. We call this look "Soft + Modern." Furnishings are familiar, not trendy. And they sit well: A little extra padding does the trick without sacrificing clean lines. **WORKS BOTH WAYS:** This is a great space for relaxing alone or with a group: The 96-inch sofa is ideal for naps; it also fits at least four at soirees. The ottoman can be a footrest or extra seats. The slipper chairs can be shared. **CONSIDER YOUR OPTIONS:** This simple modern room could suit a range of styles. ❯❯❯ See it furnished in three different but equally comfortable ways in Chapter 4.

LUSH TEXTURES. Leather and suede help form a tranquil mix. Placing seating at the center of the 24×17-foot room provides plenty of space for guests to mingle at parties. It also establishes a traffic pattern for the room, which is open to the entry, patio, and dining room. On the wall are three examples from a Southern photography collection that is a common decorating thread throughout the house.

Good flow from room to room—physically and visually—makes a house party-ready and easy to live in every day.

Opening the living room to the dining room helps it feel expansive even when accommodating dozens. A high ceiling, limited furnishings, and the space-expanding exterior glass wall also contribute. **COMFORT FACTORS:** At night recessed ceiling lights set on dimmers let us create a flattering clublike glow. By day pocket doors with frosted-glass inserts may be closed to create a cozier living area while still capturing sun from dining room windows. **SURPRISE INSIDE:** During cocktail hour, we close the doors while dinner is laid out on the dining table. Opening the doors after the table is set lets guests enjoy the full impact of the creative presentation. On nights when we entertain smaller groups without staff help, we can shut the doors and adjourn to the living room instead of having to leave our guests right away to clean up.

IT'S NOT OUR CUSTOM TO GO CUSTOM. However, here's one of those times when Bob couldn't resist. He created the dining room's glass-topped steel table and built-in sideboard, opposite, in shapes and materials that reflect the interior's calm minimalist effect. The tabletop is easy to maintain and makes the long surface look smaller and lighter. Pairing the table with chairs in soft faux suede eases any industrial feel. With their open backs, the chairs have a linear quality like the table and sideboard. In the living room, above left, a distressed-leather club chair and two ottomans heat up the cool modern scene. Beside the chair, a handmade African four-legged stool also adds warmth.

Comfort in the kitchen means having what you need where you need it. Whether you're making dinner for 50 or omelets for two, here are highlights of the good cooking life from Sean Robinson, our company chef. Allowing no more than 2 or 3 feet between sink, stove, and refrigerator sure makes cooking easier. **DOUBLE APPLIANCES ROCK:** Two sinks ease prep work; two dishwashers ensure that clean forks always are available. And you can never have enough counter space; covered in a rich-looking durable material, it also dresses up a kitchen.

WE LIKE TO WATCH: Guests often pull up counter stools while our easygoing chef and his assistants prepare feasts. We've done it too—it's like watching a ballet.

FRESH START. The original kitchen was beyond salvation (before shot, above). Even its location didn't suit entertaining, so we gutted it, converted it into the dining room, and turned the much-larger family room into cooking central. Bob designed the cabinetry, right, to include appliance garages with pull-down tambour doors that free up counter space and streamline the look. Along with the cherry cabinets, a row of amber-glass pendant lamps over the island adds warmth and gives efficient task light without getting in the way.

After playing the gracious hostess, Lulu knows exactly where to unwind.

If, like Bob, you've always wanted a canopy bed, you might think a modern setting isn't the place to make it happen. But the unfussiness of this brushed-metal version was exactly what appealed to him. Paired with a linen duvet, it suits the Soft + Modern theme of the house. For desk space, the coupling of a straight-lined brushed-metal table with a wood-legged, fabric-upholstered dining chair gives a similar effect.

SET UP A SANCTUARY: Nightly we're thankful for furnishings that help make bedrooms havens: a well-padded reading chair, a low ottoman at the end of the bed, a writing desk with plenty of surface area, and window coverings in neutral colors and natural materials that add texture and filter light.

GREAT GETAWAY. In one bedroom, opposite, an ottoman in beige chenille proves just the right height for Lulu to climb up on. The room also features a special window treatment, an easy-to-maneuver system of linen panels on tracks that looks custom-made but came from a home improvement store. In another bedroom, above right, a reading chair fits next to the bed, and the nightstand has enough room for a lamp and a drink. An unfussy version of a traditional draped table, the nightstand sports a solid-color khaki-denim skirt with a few crisp pleats.

Not a morning person? A shot of color in the bath might help. These baths let Bob get a color fix without disturbing the all-white ambience of the rest of the house. **PLAIN YET FANCY:** Handpainted imports aren't the only way to go. In one bath, Bob used readily available tiles from a home improvement center, relying on their rich hues and an original arrangement to make the room special. The contrast of blue and butter yellow with the white tiles of the shower floor and whirlpool tub looks fresh. A large window with glazed glass for privacy keeps the bath from being dark by day. **EXPECT THE UNEXPECTED:** For another bath, we searched for just the right shade of pale-blue tiles to create a spalike effect. We finally found it in swimming pool tiles and used them to enliven the wall behind the sinks.

ROUND IT OUT. Circular mirrors and raised vessel sinks, above left, have a custom feel but are actually from a home center. Note the wall-mounted faucet. High-quality hardware is one of the best investments you can make in a bath—think how often it gets used. Drawers in the cabinet improve organization. Bars on the front of the counter keep face towels handy. In another bath, opposite, the shower is designed not to need a curtain, allowing the tile to be seen and imbuing the room with a relaxing openness.

CHAPTER 3

A Little Help From Our Friends

Other people's rooms we could relax in

You know that great feeling of walking into someone's house and instantly being at home? It's like meeting a kindred spirit. On the following pages are living rooms, a dining room, and bedrooms that put us in that frame of mind. They offer insight into the art of getting comfortable.

No matter the style or the size of your rooms, there's always a way to make them comfortable.

Although Tipper and Al Gore live in Nashville, they've always kept Tipper's childhood home, built in 1938 by her grandparents, in the family. They recently asked us to update the living room, seen here and on the following pages, with a lighter feel still in keeping with the traditional spirit of the house. As people who like modern but also appreciate a nice roll arm, we understood. It led us to create a look we call "Hip Traditional." **HOW TO GET IT:** First establish a soft background, with warm neutrals for walls, carpet, and draperies. Next select comfortable furnishings with a less formal feel. The traditional sofa, for example, is more relaxed because it is slipcovered rather than upholstered. Then mix in favorite pieces. "I love the way Mitchell and Bob so easily worked in the Chippendale tables I remember as a little girl," Tipper says. The color scheme made it easy. Keeping hues neutral and fabrics mainly solid helps blend diverse furniture shapes. Finally, arrange the furniture for easy living and entertaining. Instead of a wood coffee table, use a leather bench ottoman so you can sit close or put your feet up.

CLASSIC WITH MODERN FLAIR. Using soft, solid-color prewashed linen for the sofa slipcover puts the whole room more at ease. Gold silk draperies are a simple but rich touch, drawing your eye upward so that the ceiling seems higher.

" How you furnish really makes a difference. Reducing the amount of pattern in a room and choosing soft colors that are close in tone quickly helps create a calming effect." — *Mitchell*

A busy life can bring a true appreciation of peacefulness at home. In the sitting area off the living room, we encouraged serenity by eliminating pattern, trading a damask sofa and plaid chairs for solid-color armless pieces. Replacing a tray table with two upholstered cubes brought in more quiet shapes. **MAKING IT PERSONAL:** Mounted on the bookcase are photos Tipper took during her extensive travels. The first time we visited the house, we noticed a few tiny shots on a table and wondered what they'd look like big. We blew up a few, and when we saw how great they were, it made us want to share with others Tipper's way of seeing the world. So we began offering a collection of her photography. **》》** For more Hip Traditional style, see Comfort Lesson #3, page 118.

RELAXED AND SOPHISTICATED. The armless sofa and chairs, opposite, feature a few simple button tufts that give a nod to tradition. A chenille-upholstered dining chair, like the one in the foreground, is a good way to fit one more seat into a room. As the Before photo at left shows, the newly designed room's freshness comes from furniture style and fabric changes. The layout stayed the same.

We found clean-lined country comfort and a fellow outsider art fan in the home of Sandra Soria, executive editor of *Country Home* magazine. (Note the primitive oil-on-wood painting over her fireplace.) **SMART SETUP:** Flanking the whitewashed-brick fireplace with built-in pine storage cabinets gives the room a strong focal point. It also helps achieve clutter-free calm in what is often a busy family-filled space. A conversation area centered on a round leather ottoman offers a good mix of seating: a slipcovered sofa, a pair of wing chairs, and a daybed. A well-edited and well-lit folk art display lets you appreciate each item. The room's neutral background makes the pieces stand out and keeps them from feeling fussy. **MAKING IT PERSONAL:** Some pieces, like the little red cowboy boots Sandra's eldest son once wore, are extra-special.

THE LIVING IS EASY. Balanced between family and entertaining needs, the living room features traditional furnishings with fresh shapes. Nailheads in polished nickel instead of antique brass update wing chairs that have two different looks. One wears a crisp cotton stripe, while the other is in leather with vintage fabric covering its seat cushion.

GOING NATURAL. A daybed is a good choice here. When not claimed by the family terrier, above right, it is favored by the kids because it can be shared. It's also practical: On the wall behind it is a flat-panel TV. If you're sitting on the sofa, opposite, the backless daybed ensures a clear view of your show. The room's color scheme takes its cues from natural elements, as seen in the stone-filled bamboo bowl on the wooden tray, right. Pharmacy-lamp sconces, above, are graphic elements in and of themselves and ensure that the folk art versions of the family's horses get their proper due.

For newlyweds, a nice way to begin: Start fresh by picking the basics of a room together—sofa, chairs, and accent tables. **LESS IS MORE:** Limit furnishings at first. It not only makes the job easier and less expensive but also lets you personalize with special pieces over time. **COLOR STORY:** Find harmony with a shared favorite hue like this sea blue. The sofa wears solid-blue faux suede, which is rich-looking and easy to care for. Pattern appears on smaller pieces.

TRUE BLUE. Furnishings with a contemporary feel contrast with traditional architectural elements such as paneled wainscoting and a mantel with dentil molding, opposite. White paint on walls, woodwork, and the wide-plank floor makes the furniture "pop" and helps the room feel bright, reflecting light from French doors leading to a garden. A white shag rug anchors the seating area and adds subtle texture. Used as a side table, nesting tables made of mirror and metal also reflect light. The blue-tinged base of the lamp, above, is reminiscent of sea glass. On the coffee table, left, a trio of vases is a great beginning for a collection.

Along with this living room's comfortable decor, the owners' relaxing reason for buying the cottage appeals to us. Our friends and clients Joanna and Bill Seitz travel extensively to gather goods for their home and clothing shop, J. Seitz & Co., in New Preston, Connecticut. They chose this 700-square-foot lakefront hideaway, just a few miles from their store, because it lets them reach their "vacation destination" in 15 minutes. A comfort to their busy lives, it is low-maintenance, providing them more time with their daughter, friends, and yellow Lab. **GREAT WAY TO LIVE:** Furnishings old and new have a patina that suits the cottage's vintage feel and encourages unwinding. A roll-arm sofa and armless chairs wear soft, washable white-linen slipcovers, enlivened by pillows in rosy vintage stripes and florals. A cozy wicker chair, rustic pine pieces, and a tall French iron candelabra add visually appealing texture.

FAVORITE THINGS. A photo by Bill Seitz, a professional photographer, hangs beside the windows, opposite. The Southwestern throw on the sofa recalls another of the couple's favorite spots, New Mexico. A reproduction painted-pine bench makes a practical coffee table. The white-painted wood floor has a checkerboard stenciled in soft gray to look faded. Box pleats trim easy-care slipcovers, above left.

Okay, we couldn't resist. This "dream shot" shows what we'd do with the sunroom of our renovated '50s ranch shown in Chapter 2—if we weren't using it as a second dining room for business entertaining. Call it our "retirement room." We imagine days spent reading in the sun on the U-shape pillow-back sectional, dog at our feet. After dark, this would be a media room, with movies playing on a flat-panel TV opposite the sectional. Sectionals are smart solutions for media rooms: You can stretch out or seat several. The sleek coffee table fits perfectly into the U. Clearly, Lulu approves. She looks ready to retire right now.

THE WONDERS OF WINDOW FILM. A clear protective film on the glass makes this arrangement possible, right. The film is sunscreen for furniture, blocking ultraviolet rays to stop fading. (Everything—fabric, leather, wood, art—fades if left in direct sun.) Film also reduces heat and glare. A low buffet, above, helps incorporate a TV into the room. If space permits, a storage-and-display bonanza can be created by flanking the buffet with tall bookcases.

Here's a different but equally inviting take on sectional living—modern, elegant, and soothing in its monochromatic palette. From the first time we met Drew Terrat, an interior designer and co-owner of the Mitchell Gold + Bob Williams store in Boston, we felt at home with him. Looking at his living room, it's clear that the simpatico feeling includes a mutual passion for relaxed design. **ENTERTAINING IDEAS:** With those multitasking cube ottomans, armless sofas and chairs that are easy to share, and two separate conversation areas within one big room, we can imagine some great parties here. **MAKE LIGHT OF IT:** Picture windows with modern metal mullions brighten the space by day. The windows are also focal points of the room, frames for expansive city views that look like artwork. Dimmer-controlled recessed lighting in soffits along the perimeter of the room illuminates without glare.

COME TOGETHER. Two right-arm sofas make up the sectional, a classic combination of tufted backs and bench seats, opposite. Sectionals often are sold as individual components that can be configured to best fit your space. (See Chapter 8 for more on sectionals.) In the living room's second seating area, above left, a flat-panel TV hangs over a built-in buffet cabinet.

Peri Wolfman is a true design diva. She once owned a well-known home-furnishings store in New York. Just one visit and we knew this was someone who understands comfort. **GREAT WAY TO LIVE:** White slipcovers always have been a part of her style, even with kids, dogs, and now grandkids—a testament to the covers' easy care. The living area of the loft she shares with photographer husband Charles Gold combines crisp white with natural wood for a timeless and very livable look. It features a large conversation area that includes an armless sofa and bench ottoman, each in tufted white leather. This grouping flows naturally into the dining area, where chairs in short white slipcovers surround a long pine farm table. **FEEL THE LOVE:** The loft also showcases one of Peri's collecting passions—white tableware displayed on shelves and étagères.

EVERYTHING IN ITS PLACE. Such a serene look requires good storage. Note the rows of drawers in the cabinet separating the kitchen from the dining area. The loft enjoys light from the tall windows, while flowing curtains screen sun. Complementing the wood-and-white scheme are favorite collectibles: copper cookware on the top shelf in the kitchen and silver pieces set on countertops. Many of the pieces have appeared in the pages of books on collecting by Peri Wolfman and Charles Gold.

When is a home office like a living room? For Eloise Goldman, our public relations director, it's weekday afternoons when her three sons come home from school. **SMART SETUP:** We like how she incorporates work and family with a place for the boys to do homework. (This isn't for everyone; the woman clearly has great concentration and well-behaved sons.) **TWO IN ONE:** The office has a sitting area for meetings, with a long ottoman where press kits can be spread out and reviewed. Eloise's desk faces a second desk that visiting coworkers can use when in town.

PRACTICALITY PERSONIFIED. This home office can even accommodate overnight guests. It includes a small sleeper sofa slipcovered in washable red denim, above, where Eloise enjoys a "good" time-out with sons Grant and Chase. (Oldest son Benny was away at camp.) The black, white, and red scheme of mainly solid colors is lively yet doesn't overwhelm. An antique farm sign lends personality and replays the room's hues. Portraits of the boys by Eloise's desk, right, also personalize the space. Red-trimmed desk chairs in stain-repellent stone-color faux suede and a built-in desk with pegboard over it form a homework station. A TV mounted on a bracket can be turned toward the sofa, allowing Eloise to keep up with home-design shows.

In the right room, relaxation, rejuvenation, and that sometimes-elusive deep sleep can be easier to achieve.

Wraparound windows make this second-floor master bedroom feel like a treetop retreat. **COMFORT FACTOR:** Embroidered sheers behind quilted draperies give two options for controlling the light entering the room. **LET IT SHINE:** A silver-painted dresser and nightstands add a touch of glamour. A distressed-mirror side table reflects light, making the room seem even airier. **BALANCING ACT:** The simple symmetry of matching nightstands on each side of the bed is restful to the eye. These three-drawer chests provide both closed storage and the luxury of enough space on top for alarm clocks, family photos, favorite objects, and fresh flowers.

DUAL READING SPOTS. There's a back-hugging tub chair in the corner by the window, left, with a swing-arm standing lamp and a side table beside it for coffee or a nightcap. Or you might prefer the bed, opposite, with its tall padded headboard to lean against. Note that the footboard is low enough to see over in case you want to hang a flat-panel TV on the wall opposite the bed.

It's all about the bed in this casual yet pulled-together room. The crisp white bedding with chocolate-brown trim looks so fresh and inviting. Using matching lamps and nightstands frames the bed and draws your eye to it. The lamps have white ceramic bases and linen shades that tie in to the color of the bedding. **TWO IN ONE:** At the foot of the bed, a tufted chenille ottoman stands in for a footboard and serves as a smart storage solution. It has a hinged top and cedar lining, making it ideal for storing wool sweaters in the summer.

SIMPLE BUT STRONG. The graphic design of the duvet cover, top sheet, and pillowcases makes the bed the focus of the room and lets it look well dressed even without accent pillows. The bed's fabric-upholstered padded headboard was custom-designed to fit under the window. Placing the wing chair on the diagonal helps make the space feel cozier.

PART II

Comfort Lessons
How To Make Yourself at Home

"Think of it as collecting rather than decorating. Surround yourself with pieces you love." —*Bob*

CHAPTER 4

What Furniture Can Do to a Room

One living room, three looks

As you've seen in our homes and the homes of our friends, we love a range of styles—as long as they're designed for relaxed living. To further illustrate this, we used the living room of our modern home, which you toured in Chapter 2, as our "lab." Here's how changing the furnishings transformed the room from "Slipcover Heaven" to "A Little Bit L.A." to "Soft + Modern."

NOTE: Part of our design philosophy is that everyone should have a favorite piece of furniture. So starting in this chapter, you'll find members of the Mitchell Gold + Bob Williams team pictured with their favorite and sharing what makes it great to live with.

3 Ways in the Living Room

Use these floor plans to compare furniture picks and placement.

You can tell the comfort story in any style. It's all about the pieces you choose and where you put them. The three layouts for this 24×17-foot living room suit entertaining and everyday living. They take advantage of the entire space, positioning furniture away from the walls to form multiple seating groups and clear paths through this household hub, which is open to the entry, dining room, and patio. White walls and light wood floors let furnishings convey your favorite style. Use ideas from these layouts to design a living room from scratch or to realign what you have and exchange pieces with other rooms. >>> For more tips on furniture arranging, see "Layouts for Living Rooms" in Chapter 6.

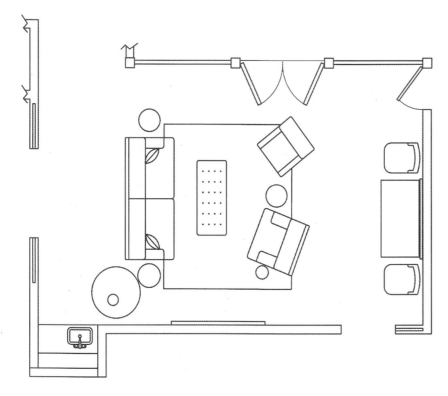

◀ LOOK 1
Slipcover Heaven

Here a big slipcovered sofa and two chairs sit across from each other, flanking the fireplace. An ottoman between them can be a coffee table or extra seats. The chairs are angled to make the group feel more casual and intimate. Behind them, smaller-scale chairs by a desk can join the seating area or be part of a home office. Traffic is well controlled: no need to walk through conversations to go from entry to patio.

LOOK 2 ▶

A Little Bit L.A.

This fun, airy look leaves floor space free for cocktail-party socializing. A long sectional with a sophisticated curve faces the fireplace. A chaise for reading by the fire has the right accoutrements: a standing lamp and side table. It also has a great view of the backyard and of a photo collection leaning on a dining-size table. The table could hold a buffet or be enlisted as another dining spot if needed.

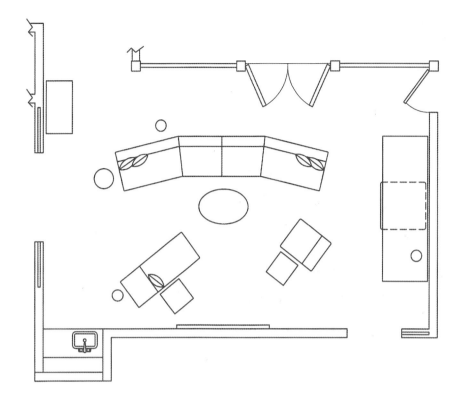

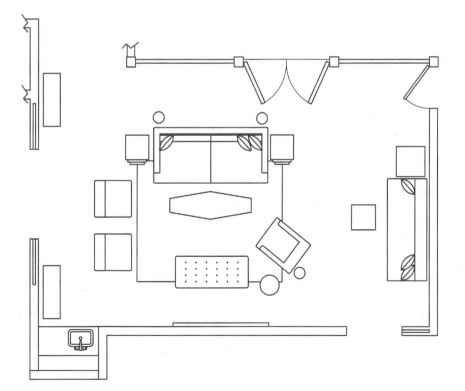

◀ **LOOK 3**

Soft + Modern

This layout has two seating areas. In the main one, a plush sofa faces the fireplace. Opposite it a bench ottoman is doubly nice: Being backless, it doesn't block your view of the fire, yet it's ready when you must seat a crowd. Armless chairs plus a wing chair complete the group. Behind the wing chair, a second sofa awaits quiet talks. Across the room, bookcases by dining room doors provide display space.

LOOK 1
Slipcover Heaven

Here's a true classic: crisp white slipcovers, rich dark wood, and soft supple leather. We haven't found a room that this style won't work well in. The furniture arrangement lets you comfortably seat a crowd or be cozy without a soul, curled up by the fire reading the Sunday paper. It also lets you enjoy fireplace or backyard views, depending on which way you lie on the sofa. Furnished this way, the room has a timeless quality that won't leave you at the whims of furniture fashion. And yet because the upholstery is slipcovered, you always have an easy opportunity for change.

MULTITASKERS. A bench-ottoman-coffee table offers extra seating. At parties we've fit as many as six on it, three to a side. Adding a finely woven rattan ottoman like the round one by the pedestal table is an affordable way to get yet another seat. It also may be moved where needed to hold a drink or snack. To balance the round ottoman and layer in more texture, we added the rustic willow hearth basket.

A good part of the room's warmth comes from the relaxed, casual slipcovers in soft prewashed white denim. Also contributing is the mix of furniture styles and materials: traditional fabric upholstery with modern-feeling leather, and rustic woven accents with wood pieces in satiny finishes. Reflective materials enrich the natural scheme too. A metal pedestal table and distressed mirror over the fireplace reflect light from a window wall across from them. The fireplace wall also would be a good spot for a flat-panel TV.

RUG CONNECTION. A striped rug anchors the seating area, right. Three types of pedestal tables add sculptural roundness to contrast with the straight-lined pieces. Frosted-glass pocket doors close off living room from dining room. Lulu, above, clearly loves a good club chair no matter what its style.

"A touch of intricate 18th-century cabinetry goes a long way. I think it's like a sculpture." —*Mitchell*

Instead of removing the "rec-room" paneling when we renovated this 1950s ranch house, we simply painted it white. This not only updated the look but also saved money, brightened the space, and added subtle design interest through the pattern of vertical lines.

A WAY WITH DISPLAY. Putting accessories on a tray, above, is a smart idea for surfaces also used for eating or seating. The pedestal table, right, sports prime examples from Mitchell's loving-cup collection. Grouping three lends visual power that one alone wouldn't have. The reproduction 18th-century chest, opposite, is a revolving exhibition space for art and objects, which helps keep the room looking fresh. (Leaning art instead of hanging it makes you much more likely to change it.) We keep objects close in color, including ephemera like the leaves, a very affordable floral alternative that brings the outdoors in. A benefit of accessorizing lightly: Details like the dresser's eight-wood inlay design and antiqued-brass hardware get equal time.

Two Options for the Far Wall

These photos show different ideas for the other side of our Slipcover Heaven living room. (This is the area directly behind the leather and slipcovered chairs.) Because we're big on parties, both of these options offer entertaining benefits. **HAVEN FOR CONVERSATION:** A second seating area, opposite, relies on armless pieces, which take up less space so the spot feels cozy, not tight. **STAGING/SERVING STATION:** When you have many guests, it helps to have a spot like the one shown above for pocketbooks and packages. Or relegate bags to the guest room and use the desk as an hors d'oeuvres station. This balanced tableau also keeps two extra pull-up chairs handy. ❯❯❯ If you like white slipcovers as much as we do, check out more examples in Comfort Lesson #1 on page 102.

TAKE YOUR PICK. A metal-trimmed mirror centers the grouping, opposite, which adds four more seats to the room. With standing lamps flanking the sofette, it is also good for reading on quiet nights. Victorian-inspired chairs, above left, look chic slipcovered. An antique trunk under the table adds storage space. At private times, the desk retrieves its role as writing spot. Lanterns add a romantic glow.

LOOK 2
A Little Bit L.A.

> **❝** I can't resist this chaise. It's like a work of art. And yet it's extremely comfortable— great for watching TV, working on my laptop, or just relaxing."
>
> —*Anne, Miami*

This was a fun switch: from traditional slipcovers to L.A. midcentury modern with a touch of glam. Again the big space is well suited to a bash but accommodates evenings alone as well. **ART CLASS:** In keeping with our goals of making a home comfortable and personal, we chose simple but interesting furniture shapes and let our collection of Southern photography become the focus of the room. This turned out to be enjoyable from more than an art standpoint. The photographs' diverse subject matter makes great conversation starters for our guests at cocktail hour.

LAID-BACK LIVING. The low-slung chaise is a visual reminder to chill. A wood frame inside makes a piece like this durable. For fireside-reading pleasure, we added a wood cube and floor lamp. A photo against the wall is easy to switch out to help give the room a new look. A table, opposite below, holds a fuller array of art ripe for rearranging.

PORSC

Woman

COLOR STORY: The room is a serene and sophisticated blend of taupe, brown, and beige accented with chalky blue. The faux-suede upholstery fabrics feel soft, and they clean easily, so you can fear light colors less. Pattern is subtle, as in the checkerboard rug, or restricted to accents, as on the striped pillows.

GREAT SHAPE. The curving midcentury sectional is the first thing you see when you walk in the door. Its shape looks inviting. This is actually two sofas that span 15 feet—a party-oriented option if you can fit it in. The sofas also would look good facing each other.

Transition Wall: Two Views

When a living room opens to a dining room, what goes on the partial wall in between? Here are two pieces that suit our A Little Bit L.A. look. Both are special enough for a spot that gets noticed and practical enough for the functions of the room. **MIRRORED IMAGE:** A study in glamour, the antiqued-mirror chest on the opposite page makes a great bar cabinet. Dark walnut trim picks up the woods in the living and dining rooms. A mirror reflects light from the fireplace and outdoors. When we serve buffet-style, guests rest their drinks on the chest while getting food. **WARM WOOD:** The glass-front 1940s-style cherry cabinet above connects well with both rooms. Books, barware, and collectibles find a home here. ⟫ L.A. modern style can deliver many looks. For another take, see Comfort Lesson #8 on page 140.

'50s FLAVOR. Here it comes from upholstered chairs with bare midriffs, above left and opposite. Their shape recalls folding chairs from bridge-table sets so key to "Happy Days" entertaining. Legs are stained coffee-bean brown, and upholstery is practical chocolate-color faux suede, also used on the armless chair in the living room. The chairs contrast nicely with the white walls and lighter wood floors.

LOOK 3
Soft + Modern

For us, "modern" and "comfortable" are totally compatible. We look to the modern style of the 1940s and 1950s for ideas. Here's how to make this Soft + Modern version of the living room inviting on several levels. **VISUALLY:** Use natural materials, accented with solid colors instead of patterns, for a soothing look. Select modern furniture that is classic, not jagged and artsy for art's sake. Mix in a few traditional upholstery pieces, such as a wing chair, but update them by choosing solid, unexpected colors. **TO THE TOUCH:** Select furniture in materials that feel good: broken-in leathers, satiny wood finishes, plush fabrics. **BY THE "SIT":** Give upholstery the "tush test." Sit on it and check that it is well padded where it counts—in the seat, where your back touches it, and where you rest your arms and head. **FOR EASY LIVING:** Reduce clutter by limiting accessories. This makes a room appealing for parties because there's less to knock over. It also conjures calmness and makes home maintenance easier. ⟫⟫ For more Soft + Modern, see Comfort Lesson #2 on page 110.

BETTER TOGETHER. We like the subtle mix of colors and textures, opposite. The wood grain of the simple cubes becomes a decorative element. Tufting on the armless love seat adds a graphic note. The soft beige throw, subtly textured russet pillow, and glowing amber-glass vase layer on more contrast. Even the background, a white-painted paneled wall, contributes. The coffee table, above left, warmly expresses modern style. It has graceful cabriole legs connected by stretchers for extra support.

Wherever you sit in this room, you get interesting views: backyard, fireplace, or photo wall. Rich materials, including avocado-green and spice-red leather, enliven the scene. Displaying a personal passion on walls—such as Southern photography—individualizes a space without cluttering it. **WELL PLACED:** To make the most of the large room, we pulled upholstered pieces away from the walls. If you "float" pieces like this, be sure they are well finished on all sides; this is a hallmark of quality furniture. Floating furniture also directs traffic through the room to the entry, patio, and dining room. When arranging furniture in a room with multiple entries, make sure it looks balanced from each view.

MADE FOR ENTERTAINING. The furniture arrangement forms great conversation areas that can be divided into smaller chat spots. The ottoman is a good choice for that spot because it doesn't block views of the fireplace. Nesting tables serve as side tables for the sofa; guests appreciate them at big buffet dinners.

Continuing the spice-tone scheme from living to dining room ensures a smooth visual transition that feels tranquil. In the dining room, high-back chairs in persimmon velvet bring out warm tones in the clean-lined wood table. A wood bookcase flanking the doorway shows an arrangement of books and collectibles. Large items dominate two of the shelves for visual impact and a more open feeling.

SIMPLE SHAPES, RICH DETAILS. Buttonless grid tufting highlights the leather ottoman above. Polished-nickel nailheads outline the leather sofa, and contrast welt trims the pillows, right. Sisal rugs define furniture groupings in the living room and dining room, opposite.

CHAPTER 5

Create Comfort To Suit Your Style

A stressless way to discover which furnishings you like

Find furniture shopping stressful? It doesn't have to be. Learn which types of pieces are right for you before you go. These 15 "Comfort Lessons" will help you identify your preferences in the low-pressure atmosphere of your own home. See what it takes to create relaxing rooms in a variety of styles. Remake styles such as country or modern in fresh ways with unexpected blends of shapes, textures, and colors. **HOW TO USE THE LESSONS:** Each lesson includes furniture arrangements against simple backgrounds instead of in decorated rooms to reduce distractions and let you focus on the furnishings. First browse the chapter, noting groupings that catch your eye. Jot down page numbers or bookmark them. Trust your gut. Love it? Mark it. Next, read about the groupings. Do they have a style or color in common? Or maybe you like pieces from several lessons—a perfect start to your own mix. Last, review your favorite groupings to see if they suit your room's functions or if you must change or add pieces.

1. Wood + White, Always Right

We would never sacrifice comfort for sophistication. Believe us, you don't have to. Dark wood furniture and crisp white upholstery give you both. Associated with restful beach resorts in the Caribbean, this pairing conveys tradition while still looking fresh and modern. It's hard to imagine anything more soothing to the eye. **GREAT WAY TO LIVE:** This approach can blend diverse elements, so you can incorporate furniture you already own, such as family pieces from different eras. It also enhances a room with a view by putting the emphasis on the outdoors. **EMBRACE CHANGE:** Choose this calm and classic background to show off colorful collectibles or introduce a few hues through pillows, lamps, and throws. Then change and rearrange those pieces for an affordable and fun way to give a room new life. You even could change your slipcovers. **EVERYDAY LUXURY:** Washable white denim slipcovers are chic and easy-care. You can bleach them, which means less worry about stains, and they get softer with each washing.

CLASSIC COMFORT. A coffee table with burled-walnut veneers and detailed turnings, above left, has grain patterns that warm a room and please the eye. The table, opposite, holds a vase of peonies—Mitchell's favorite flowers "because they're beautiful without being overpowering and remind me of the pushed-in faces of bulldogs like my Lulu." The arrangement is lush yet low enough to allow clear views across the table.

FOR SERENITY CUT CLUTTER.
Armoires can help. There's
also something to be said for
a special piece, antique or
instant heirloom, to preserve
family history or start a
tradition. This reproduction's
doors have "book-matched"
veneers: wood sliced super-
thin, then opened like a book
and applied, creating mirror
images.

ISN'T IT INVITING? This is
a "shelter" sofa, meaning
arms are the same height as
the back. It's also a "scatter-
back," with a row of plump
pillows to adjust for
comfort. Although elegant
in its tailored slipcover, it's
easy care. Velcro inside the
slipcover below the arms
shows off the curves and
keeps things neat.

> " The reality is that some people have back problems. Help make everybody comfortable by varying seating in a room. Here there's a sofa for lounging but also a well-padded armless chair and an upright chair with arms. Take your pick." —*Mitchell*

MY TURN. The turned legs of the table add "pop" to this setting. That's the beauty of Wood + White: It gives an unusual piece the attention it deserves without detracting from the overall calm.

LEAN BACK. A rattan chair is especially comfortable because its back has "give." Enhancing the sit is a padded cushion in soft prewashed white denim, which links the chair to the upholstered seating pieces.

Variation on the Theme

Here we augment the Wood + White mix with classic ticking stripes, medium wood tones, and a modern chandelier. **COMFORT FACTOR:** Upholstered dining chairs are truly friends with benefits. They let you relax at the table for hours. And they can introduce pattern or color to a room

SIZE MATTERS. You'll never regret a table that extends. This updated country French table with cabriole legs starts at card-table size, above right, but has self-storing leaves that pull out from each end. For an attractive alternative to a breakfront, opposite, try using a bedroom piece or family heirloom like the 18th-century reproduction chest. This can save money in what is usually an expensive room to furnish.

dominated by wood. **FASHIONABLY GREAT:** Like summer dresses, white slipcovers soften the scene. We could have put them on all four chairs but liked the effect of mixing white with a fresh ticking stripe. Dressed as they are and as comfortable as they are, the chairs can be carried into a Wood + White living room like the one on the previous pages for extra seating any time company comes.

Tuck in a Desk

Who says a home office needs a room of its own? A desk and étagère or an "executive assistant" (our p.c. name for a secretary) can fit in a corner of a living room, dining room, bedroom, or nook. **A NEW DAY:** With so many people using laptops instead of desktops, there's less need to house a bulky hard drive, so an executive assistant or writing desk with comfy chair can work. **A PLACE FOR EVERYTHING:** We keep things simple with clean-lined storage boxes on the étagère shelves. But wouldn't this be a great spot for a colorful collection to inspire your work? Also note the side table on casters, opposite, that helps keep the desktop clear. **MIXED MEDIA:** Modern in material and traditional in form, the side table bridges styles. Its metal legs repeat the turnings of the desk and étagère, while its material links with the polished-nickel lamps.

" I live in a small city apartment. When I saw this, I knew it would be the perfect home office for me. It reminds me of the secretary we had when I was a little girl. I call it my executive assistant." –*Julie, with Gwenna, New York*

ELEGANT ALTERNATIVES. Used instead of office chairs, dining chairs keep the at-home feel. A short slipcover shows off the chair's legs, opposite. Soft to the touch, the blue faux suede on the chair, above left, adds color to a room. The chair coverings are easy-care: The prewashed white denim slipcover is machine-washable, and faux suede is known for scrubbability.

2. Soft + Modern

Can modern be comfortable? Absolutely. (Doesn't the guy on the sofa look comfy?) We call our version "Soft + Modern." Shapes are streamlined without being hard-edged. Upholstery is well padded. Warmth comes from materials like hand-pleasing fabrics in neutral beige, cream, and caramel hues, as well as leather and wood. **WHAT INSPIRES US:** We're influenced by things we've seen all over the world, in particular the modern styles of France and Asia and wonderful modern classics from California. We've found that when you mix these things together, it becomes quintessential American design—after all, America is a design melting pot too. **LIKE VENUS DE MILO:** An armless sofa can be beautiful. It offers clean lines and a smaller "footprint" for tight spaces. Comfort comes from a back well pitched for lumbar support. If you crave more cushiness, you always could invoke the mix and add a soft but clean-lined slipcovered chaise to the room.

❝ I love this sofa because it's so L.A., and I'm from L.A. The leather makes it striking— soft and modern, yet swanky."
– Erick, Newport Beach, California

TUFT LOVE. Lushness comes from textural contrasts, such as sleek leather and distressed velvet, opposite. Subtle contrast also shows in the tufting—buttoned on the pillow and buttonless on the sofa. Tufting suits these materials. Stretching and tucking leather creates natural variations in tone and gives velvet depth by multiplying the surfaces off which light can play.

SET TO SNOOZE. Lulu enjoys the cool comfort of leather when she first lies down and loves how it warms to her body as she dozes. We can relate. We like leathers "aniline dyed," which means the dye goes all the way through. This adds suppleness and, if the surface is scratched, it doesn't show unsightly white underneath, as do "painted" leathers, which are only surface-coated. That's good news for dogs that jump on sofas.

MAKE LIGHT OF IT. The lamp brings welcome roundness to an angular setting, and its height establishes a visual middle ground between the tall bookcase and low seating. It's large enough to cast reading light for two. With its appealing organic form, it's both accessory and necessity.

Calm is comfortable, as this hip modern arrangement shows. **BALANCING ACT:** This is how color maintains balance. Lighter hues have more visual weight, although the darker objects are more massive. Thus lamp and chair balance bookcase, making it feel less dominant. **A LITTLE IS A LOT:** We usually use solid fabrics because patterns have big visual impact, which can be jarring. Try smaller patterns with colors close in range like the cubed geometric on the chair. **SIZE-WISE:** The cube before the sofa is a smart coffee-table option: It doesn't block the whole sofa, so you can get up easily, and it may be shifted left or right as needed.

The straight lines of the modern chandelier mirror those of the dining table, glass-front cabinet, and upholstered chairs. The rectangular chandelier directs light the length of the table, giving all diners a clear view of their plates.

PRETTY FACE. Consider a cabinet, like this one with dark-cherry veneers, against the wall as a chic stand-in for a traditional sideboard. Sliding glass doors and a light natural-cherry interior suit the cabinet for storage or display; the top can hold a favorite collection or be a convenient serving surface.

Repetition of the beige, brown, and green scheme helps pair this dining room with the living room on the previous pages. Limiting colors and choosing unadorned classics for furnishings lets you personalize with accessories. **MIX MASTERED:** Simple wood tables have a place in modern settings. Their design feels current. And because they suit so many decors, it's easy to imagine the tables being passed down, making appearances in many eras.

An upholstered headboard in the bedroom epitomizes our Soft + Modern style. In addition to comfort, it introduces soothing color like this pale blue. Here textures are the "patterns" in the room: woodgrain, mottled leather, nubby chenille. **LAYER IT ON:** White accents—sheets, lampshade, frames for family photos—add freshness.

WHAT'S IN A NIGHTSTAND? How great to have display space, an open shelf, and drawers so that not everything is public knowledge. The chest of richly grained quartersawn oak, above, has a low-maintenance glass top and wood "lip" to prevent roll-offs. We love pieces with a story. This chest's aged-iron pulls, right, look like miniature sculptures and were handmade by an artisan at the foot of the Italian Alps. When shopping, ask about a piece's inspiration or special features. The story might cement your connection to the piece and help you personalize your home.

GOOD FOR YOUR HEAD. This kind of headboard is pure pleasure when you're reading in bed. At almost 6 feet high, the headboard becomes an architectural element. It also can divide a space. Set away from a wall and backed with a desk, it forms an office alcove. A footboard gives a finished look; be sure it's low enough to see TV over.

NOW THAT'S COMFORT. A chair in your bedroom gives you a place to slip on your socks and a temporary clothes drop (as long as you can be trusted not to let it get out of hand). The leather's color picks up the nightstand's wood tones. Its smooth surface counters the textured chenille on the bed.

3. Hip Traditional

> **I love how at first glance this chair looks traditional, but on further review you can see how subtly modern it is. That's my style, modern meets antique.**
> — *Travis, Atlanta*

Not at home in fussy rooms yet find yourself lusting after tufting? Welcome to Hip Traditional. **GETTING IT:** Use solid fabrics on upholstery shapes you probably last saw in plaid or chintz. Pick traditional pieces with a twist: a wing chair with legs that are tapered instead of turned, a pedestal table in metal instead of wood. **TYING IT TOGETHER:** Tonal hues create harmony. Use white for accents: a lampshade, pillows, hyacinths, candles, an alabaster bowl. Wood furnishings share a dark painted finish that unifies their styles. This scheme gives a room long decorating life and suits it to a changing display of photos and art.

SNAPSHOT OF A MIX.
This is not your mother's traditional. The sofa arm and armoire molding say tradition, but the linen, rustic table, and modern vase soften the formality. For us a cast-iron bulldog, opposite, personalizes the scene. What's your sign?

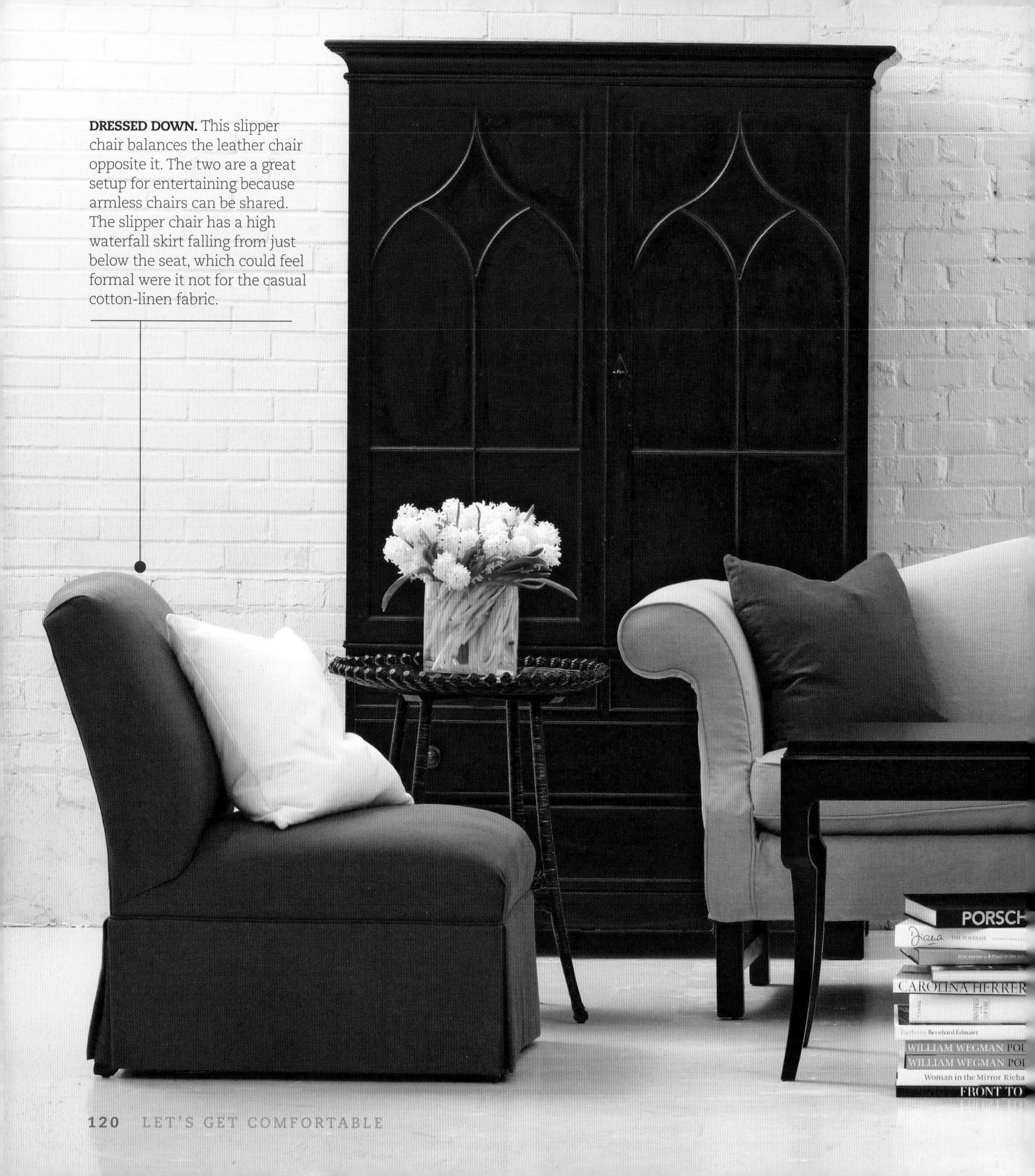
PORSCH
Diana THE PORTRAIT
CAROLINA HERRER
Bernhard Edmaier
WILLIAM WEGMAN POI
WILLIAM WEGMAN POI
Woman in the Mirror Richa
FRONT TO

DRESSED DOWN. This slipper chair balances the leather chair opposite it. The two are a great setup for entertaining because armless chairs can be shared. The slipper chair has a high waterfall skirt falling from just below the seat, which could feel formal were it not for the casual cotton-linen fabric.

HIGH STYLE. An Asian-inspired high tea table is graceful before the sofa. This 19th-century innovation let ladies serve tea without bending over, a real plus in the age of corsets. We appreciate its height too: Eating in front of the tube is much neater. So is putting drinks down at cocktail parties.

THE CAMELBACK GOES MODERN. A linen slipcover and straight legs rather than curved do the trick. It also has only side stretchers, the wood rails between front and back legs, skipping the traditional one in front. A bench seat adds to the streamlined look and keeps comfort a priority.

" Beautifully balanced, this mix is one of our favorites. Each piece is distinctive, yet none steals the show. Individually they look traditional, yet together they have a decidedly updated, original, and inviting style."
—Bob

Adding More Modern to the Mix

On the previous pages, we cloaked traditional shapes in modern dressings. Here tradition gets hipper with modern elements like the dining chairs and chandelier. **TABLE TALK:** A 19th-century Empire table with four-column pedestal base doesn't need matching chairs. Comfortable parsons

chairs, with tweed upholstery, nickel-capped legs, and nailhead trim, eliminate any hint of stodginess. The table is a regal example of workmanship from Italy. Notice the deep apron with bull-nose trim, where woodgrain runs in vertical tiger stripes. **LET IT SHINE:** A mirror leaned against a wall (or fastened to the wall if children live in the house) visually expands a space. This one, in classic Venetian style with scoring, glass rosettes, and an antiqued finish, joins the metallic elements in reflecting light.

CARRIED AWAY. The metal side table, seen in the living room on pages 20 and 82, also can help out in the dining room, opposite. The tabletop, left, a pie-cut cherry veneer with antiqued hand-waxed finish, glows. A fine finish is a pleasure to run your hand over; it feels almost soft to the touch.

"If a room gets too busy, nothing looks special. Keeping it simple lets the wonderful details stand out." —*Mitchell*

BET THE ORIGINAL WAS SPECIAL TO SOMEONE.
Based on a 1600s Dutch farmhouse piece, this cabinet has old-time practicality. When shopping for a breakfront alternative, look for a display or serving surface, drawers for silverware, and space for large pieces.

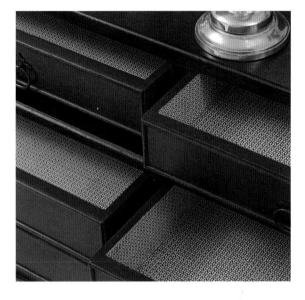

ROUND IT OUT. At 2 feet in diameter, the circular mirror is well sized to sit over the cabinet. Its dot pattern, etched on back, is flat to the touch. The chairs' nailhead trim replicates the dot pattern in miniature. Roundness also reigns in the accessories and drawer pulls.

Here's to soothing symmetry and vintage wood. We envision this tableau accompanying the previous pages' dining group, supplying storage and a spot for extra chairs. **MR. VERSATILE:** An arrangement like this also could enhance a foyer or an upstairs hall. The chest and mirror also would work in a bedroom. **SURPRISE INSIDE:** What a great tradition—lined drawers, above. These have hand-blocked Italian wallpaper applied with wallpaper paste. You can line drawers yourself "sort of" easily.

4. Serenity in the Master Suite

It's not always easy to exercise restraint, but it sure is worth it. Consider what you can achieve with white and one other hue. **COLOR STORY:** We went with blue, whose calming properties are legendary. Blue and white are timeless and work in modern or traditional decors. The pairing adds another layer to the welcoming Wood + White theme we love. **SET UP A SANCTUARY:** From a comfort standpoint, don't let furnishing your bedroom fall to last place behind the public rooms. Start by thinking of the functions the room will serve. Limit colors and don't overfurnish or overaccessorize so the space will be easy to maintain. And don't sacrifice serenity by letting the room become a dumping ground, the place you "temporarily" put things when company comes. Plan for enough storage elsewhere.

NOTICE THE DETAILS. Every chance you get, build in subtle design interest. Think soft contrasts in fabric textures and upholstery details. Here a white denim pillow is crisp against tufted cotton-linen on a sofa. For a sophisticated accent to blue and white, try mirrored pieces like the table, opposite. And nothing personalizes a room like family photos, opposite above, which are refreshing in white frames.

WHAT A TREAT. A bedside table with room for photos, lamp, books, and glass is luxury. (If you've ever lived with a tiny table, you know what we mean.) This one is 40 inches wide to give you an idea of the kind of real estate we're talking about.

IMAGINE YOUR DREAMS IN IT. This four-poster reflects the romance of 17th-century Moorish design. This is what we mean by "finding a piece you'll fall in love with." With wood finishes, it's not only the look but also the touch that's important. It should feel great as you run your hand over it on your way back to bed in the dark.

HAVE A SEAT. An end-of-bed bench lets you sit while you dress. It's also a good spot for decorative pillows at night. This one shares the bed's romance, and its curved back plays off the curved headboard.

SHINING EXAMPLE. Mirror makes this sizable piece, which offers plenty of closed storage, seem slimmer. Seek out furniture with great details. This chest has dark walnut trim that complements the bed, a double set of tapered front legs, and tiny walnut washers accenting the mirrored knobs.

With its intricate turnings, this four-poster takes center stage. To balance it, use strong shapes with simple details like the pedestal table, mirrored chest, and bench. The perfect companion to this romantic fantasy? A mirrored vanity with wood legs to keep it from getting too sweet. **BALANCING ACT:** Bob notes, "Even when I'm decorating around a color, it still comes back to balance. I'll say, 'I put blue there, now what do I need to balance it?'" Here the slipcovered bench began the process, followed by pillows and the vanity chair.

POWER SEATING. Chairs that look small but sit big are always good finds. Look for ones with supportive backs and wide seats. We call them "pull-ups" because you can bring them into a conversation area, especially if they're on casters. Front casters are enough—just tilt and roll, and the rest of the time the chair stays in place.

Want true luxury daily? Include a sitting area in your bedroom. This private and peaceful arrangement continues the luxe feel of furnishings with history in a blue-and-white scheme.

SOFA CHIC. Called a Chesterfield, this sofa style recalls more formal Edwardian times and is often done in leather or velvet. Here an unexpected fabric takes the sofa down a notch. Often, both seats and backs are tufted, but without seat tufting, the piece looks more modern. Check a Chesterfield for well-padded arms and inside corners of the back to ensure comfort.

Sleek sophistication. The Art Deco-inspired mirrored table with light-reflecting finish, above and opposite, definitely has something to do with it. **ALTERNATIVE REALITY:** For small spaces, swap the sofa for a love seat or two chairs with a table between them. This arrangement also could be the bones of a great living room. Or trade the armoire for an "executive assistant" (secretary), and you'll have a study that will almost make you glad you brought work home.

5. Comfortable Cottage

Cottage without kitsch or clutter—that's what we're after. What gives a fresh twist? Traditional pieces rendered unpredictable by fabric choice. Furniture details fun for your eye. And all of it balanced in shape, color, placement, and style.

LOVE YOUR IMPERFECTIONS: We want things relaxed, not perfect. That's why we like our woods and leathers distressed. We don't want to worry about us, our pets, or our guests making the first mark. It's an easygoing way to live. Even a new piece looks better with slight distressing; it will seem more authentic and more loved.

> **Why this chair? Nostalgia. In my 20s I lived in Paris and saw leather chairs like this in apartments, restaurants, clubs. Sometimes I sit in it, shut my eyes, and remember some very good times."**
> — *Ed, New York*

COMFORT FOR ALL. A closer look shows this cottagey print's modern theme. Called "Equal Love," it gives equal time to all kinds of couples. A tea table with undulating trim, opposite, is a sure sign of Granny's place. (But would she have served you takeout in front of the TV?) Just like Granny to make the wise choice: a coffee table with shelf beneath.

CLEAN YET CLASSIC. Roll arms, turned legs, and a crescent back characterize this English manor-house escapee with a regal profile. This kind of chair sits low, so there's no need for an ottoman—just stretch out your legs. The slim scale means it works well in pairs. We'd like two facing a fire.

NO PATTERN HERE. The Chesterfield-style sofa looks refreshingly modern in its crème cover. Also updating it are block feet instead of turned. Nailheads in two sizes add an interesting design detail. Pillows pull the color scheme together.

" Families of all stripes would feel welcome in this modern take on cottage style. The furnishings seem assembled over generations as the contents of cottages usually are." —*Mitchell*

LOTTA OTTOMAN. The semiattached top looks loose but stays neatly in place. Pull the piece up to the table or push the table aside and position the ottoman for couch sitters' feet. In this calm setting bold nailheads become eye-catching graphics.

6. Modern English

Warm neutrals. A sofa so inviting. This setting for domestic bliss follows our rule of no more than four hues in a room, with most being accents. And what versatility: All it took were pillows, a throw, and backyard branches to say "fall." Winter, spring, and summer should be a breeze.

CRÈME DE LA CRÈME. Crème welt—fabric-wrapped cording—highlights the sofa's appealing shape. It has sink-in cushions, a high angled back to lean your head against, and low pleated arms known as "English arms" or "Charles of London arms." Pillow-topped, they become headrests when you recline. English-arm sofas usually sport skirts; without one, this version feels fresh. The three-over-three cushions let someone sit comfortably in the middle.

UP YOUR OPTIONS. These tables, which include shelving for storage and display, recall those designed in the '70s by Jackie O's legendary decorator Billy Baldwin.Their shapes put the focus on the woodgrain and have an openness that helps lighten a room. Rectangular tables relate to ovals here, thanks to slender lines and similar woodtones.

GREAT IDEA. An upholstered dining chair in the living room works well with the compactness of the sofa and coffee table. A stripe gives the chair more visual weight and supplies just enough pattern for a stripped-down country feel.

7. Calm, Cool, and Collected

This is our kind of country. Soft colors. Minimal pattern. Relaxed slipcovered upholstery and wood pieces that look both sophisticated and handcrafted. Interest comes from the details—the wicker "lace" of a Victorian side table, the "turned" metal of a coffee table.

SAVVY STYLE. When designers say "classic traditional sofa," they often mean a two-seater with roll arms and a kick-pleat skirt. At 83 inches wide, this one is fine for two, the most who usually sit on any sofa at once. This is a good spot for a sofa bed: The coffee table is on casters and is easy to move aside.

SHOW YOUR STUFF. A weathered-white painted chest has just the right tones to set off pieces of McCoy pottery that we started collecting in the 1980s.

SUPPORTING ROLE. Note the profile of this classic modern shape. This is a "tightback" (no back pillow). Well-padded tightbacks give comfort and support. Need a chair that's narrow and roomy? Try one with slim "track" arms like this. Note how the geometric print picks up the woodtones. Its small scale almost reads like a texture.

CENTERPIECE. The surfboard shape of this '50s L.A.-inspired table works well with a long sofa. Wood pieces add an unusual note to a room because of their one-of-a-kind grain patterns.

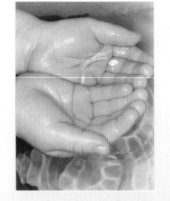

LONG AND LOW. This sofa has one big bench seat, which is great for stretching out on. A light-color welt emphasizes its sleek shape and ties it to the background of the chair's print. The dark wood base links to the tables.

8. Left-Coast Mix

Casual but with a lot of attitude. Authentic—as if it has been here for years. Open to collectibles of all kinds. Each piece holds its own, and it still all holds together. You could call it midcentury modern. We call it marvelous.

PORSCHE 911

WILLIAM WEGMAN POLAROIDS

SPOOLS 'R STOOLS. Red-painted wicker stools add texture, introduce roundness, and suit the fun mood. They give people sitting on the sectional a place for drinks. And they can be extra seats. For wicker sturdy enough to sit on, pick pieces with wood frames inside.

LOVE RED. It's bursting with personality. A setting like this doesn't need much else—just a few accents such as kiwi, butter, and white pillows and the geometric cube with '70s lamp. And if you wake up one day "over" red, you can always get a new slipcover.

9. Sectional Living

This is a kid's paradise. We'd have loved to have grown up on a sectional like this. At least now we can enjoy entertaining on it. It sits low like club furniture. You really can slouch into it. And it's slipcovered so there's no need to grow up and keep your feet off it.

UNDER THE INFLUENCE.
Straight arms and tapered legs
bring a French modern feel to
a camelback style. Soothing
color and graceful curves
provide visual comfort. Soft
cushions and pleasing seat
depth give a relaxed sit.

CALMNESS BRINGS CLARITY.
In a serene scene, little things catch your eye, such as square knobs on the drawers. And the piecrust apron: Inspiration for it came from Bob's memory of an old Texas farmhouse baking table.

10. Strength in Unity

Here and on the next two pages are two ways to create the core of a mix with your sofa, chair, and occasional tables. Once you select those elements, you'll have a major part of your living room decisionmaking done and a style, color, and spatial framework to build on. This example shows a mix built from matching pieces (sofa and chair, coffee and side tables). **GREAT SHAPE:** Not any matched set will do. Matched pieces are calming to the eye when they are a beautiful shape and a simple color. You could still layer in a subtle mix of lamps and accessories. Against this tranquil background, even the most delicate collectibles would stand out. A silver collection, for instance, would shine.

11. Beauty in Diversity

The relationship between sofa, chair, and tables can be a microcosm of a room. Find what suits you and expand from there. Unlike the mix on the previous pages, done with matching pieces, this one blends several styles. **NEVER SAY NEVER:** A modern shelter sofa with an 18th-century wing chair? It's not only for decorators. The mix will work for you, too, thanks to the high backs, coverings in the same tonal family, and "outlines" in welt and nailheads, which help the pieces read as interesting shapes rather than specific styles. **ELEMENTS IN COMMON:** Two pieces have turned legs. Two are in leathers close in tone to the wood table. The sofa has flared arms; the table, flared legs. **MR. VERSATILE:** Here's one of our favorite coffee-table solutions: a leather bench ottoman. Put your feet up without a care, take a seat, or put down a tray and serve. A rectangle like this can be shared by sofa and chair.

NOTICE THE DETAILS.
Doodads give these pieces
a dressier feel: brass
ferrules on the ottoman,
nailheads on the chair,
turnings on the table, and
welt on the sofa, which
gives it more presence and
helps balance it against
the three dark pieces.

YESTERDAY AND TODAY. A modern lamp sits serenely on an 18th-century chest, balanced by the white-framed photo behind it. Notice the photo of our lovely Lulu alongside. Judging from the effect of the chalky-blue panel behind the bed, this arrangement could be a knockout in a white room with one wall painted blue.

12. Clean Sleep

We like a little variety in the bedroom(!). The Asian-inspired four-poster and English chest and chair make a room feel collected rather than decorated all at once. **COLOR STORY:** Kiwi on the chair modernizes it instantly. (See for yourself. It's in traditional leather on pages 118 and 121.) **BEAUTIFUL DREAMER:** The romance of four-posters is undeniable. This rattan one combines solid woven panels with openwork patterns that help a big piece seem less massive. Its tones repeat those of the wood-inlay chest designs.

13. Mastering the Suite

Devastatingly handsome and easy to live with—who doesn't want that? This sophisticated masculine mix is definitely not just for men. **COLOR STORY:** A brown-and-white scheme with metallic accents gives simple elegance to the master suite on this and the following pages. An espresso-color handwoven wool rug helps unify the traditional and modern furnishings. A pillow on the settee is the only pattern; the menswear pinstripe adds a warm note. **TALL TALE:** The 5-foot-tall walnut-veneered linen cabinet offers good storage and adds height to the arrangement.

Here it appears even taller, thanks to the vases on top. Balancing the cabinet is a trio of photos by former Second Lady Tipper Gore. The arrangement fits neatly in the space formed by the cabinet and the settee to become a focal point for the seating area.

SEAT FOR TWO. Try a settee in spaces where a sofa won't fit. Upholstering this traditional form in white denim gives it a modern air, opposite. Brass nailheads along its front rail feel decorative in the spare setting and help tie it to the bronze pedestal table. Nailheads subtly link the two areas of the suite; they appear again on the headboard of the bed on the following pages.

If you're spending eight hours somewhere, make it comfortable. Invest in a great mattress that feels right to you. Buy quality bedding. Nothing feels more luxurious than crisp cotton with a reasonably high thread count. We prefer white—it goes with everything and fits the serenity mode. **EVERYDAY LUXURY:** A special touch you can't see here is the down featherbed under the fitted sheet. Synthetics work, too, if you're allergic to down.

LAYERS OF TEXTURE. Distressed leather, right, offers warmth like vintage wood. Each hide has unique natural markings, such as wrinkles, scratches, and occasionally brands. Atop the '50s-modern-inspired eight-drawer chest, opposite, a balanced tableau includes photos whose framing mirrors the white nailhead-trimmed headboard. The arrangement features handcrafted stoneware vases, above, in subtle matte finishes that recall 1940s Scandinavian pottery. Beside the vases, a lamp with a full-range dimmer allows light levels to be customized. The lamp has a patinaed bronze base and a shade in lustrous antique-gold douppioni, a nubby silk often woven from two thread colors, which makes it shimmer in the light.

WHERE'S THE BOX SPRING? This platform bed has a box spring built into its fabric-covered base so you only need a mattress to complete it. A simple white bed has its benefits: It appears to take up less space, making a room feel larger. It looks luxurious, especially with nailheads dressing it up like jewelry. And it lets you easily change bedding color or style, a fast way to revitalize your decor.

14. Pretty in Print

We've always been intrigued by toile. Here's how to use a toile-inspired fabric without making a room feel overdone.
1. Put it on a classic clean-lined piece that you want to make the focus of the room. This bed, with its gently curved camelback and mere five button tufts, is an ideal candidate. **2.** Make it the only print in the room. **3.** Use colors to softly complement those found in the print.
4. Keep accessories minimal, simple, and in either a color from the print or a natural material like wood or silver.

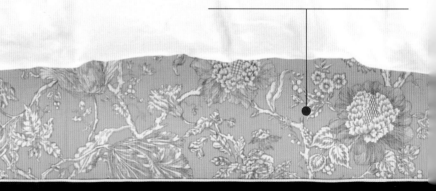

IT HAS A HISTORY. Toile is the name of the fabric that inspired this print. It comes from the French word for cloth. Toiles were first made in 1760 for the Palace of Versailles. The fabric usually depicts scenes, but this print is a "tree of life" design. Note the decorative pillow that features a welt and buttons in the same print.

SCREENED IN. Another layer of pattern comes from the Asian modern four-panel rattan screen with two types of Chinese Chippendale fretwork, tighter on top and more open on the bottom. A screen is another good way to add height to a space. It also can contribute a sense of architecture. And it can serve as a room divider, hiding a bedroom workspace during downtime.

15. Asian Fusion

A writing table in the bedroom is the height of civilized chic, even if it's for keyboarding rather than quill dipping. The bedroom on these and the following pages takes its cue from fusion cooking and blends elements of different origins into a flavorful new mix. **LOVELY TO LOOK AT:** An Asian-inspired floral, a French modern saber-leg desk, and a Chinese Chippendale chair all have graceful lines that create visual comfort. **FABRIC OF OUR LIVES:** We like florals but are always looking for ones that aren't too sweet—and keep debating whether we'll love them long-term. This red-and-black blooming-branch print has a handpainted feel and a graphic quality that lends Eastern influence without clichés. To keep the peacefulness, stick with one floral per room and use it sparingly. A print in a room full of solids has a lot of visual weight, so items must be placed carefully to avoid upsetting the balance in a tranquil space.

CONSIDER YOUR OPTIONS. In addition to a bedroom, the arrangement, opposite, could suit a serene and sophisticated home office or turn a landing into a study space. The ottoman under the desk could hold books and papers. The rattan chair features Chinese Chippendale fretwork, a style that debuted in 18th-century England. The photographs, *Rainy Shanghai* and *Beijing Girl* by Tipper Gore, also contribute Eastern flavor. To add storage and a tall element, consider an armoire like the mahogany one, above left. Based on a French modern piece, it has a rattan inlay that also subtly invokes the Orient.

Asian in its simplicity, the nightstand makes its cultural point with its design rather than its hardware. The piece has a clever pullout shelf just below the top to expand surface space. **TIES THAT BIND:** Woods, leathers, platform-bed upholstery, and even picture frames are all dark. White bed linens add crisp contrast. And just two small pillows effectively link the bed to the chair as well as to the ottoman and pillow in the desk area shown on the previous pages.

PAMPERED AND PROTECTED. Like a wing chair, the wing-back headboard of this platform bed feels sheltering. The well-padded headboard is great to lean on, and the fresh-looking white linens invite curling up. At the foot of the bed, two round ottomans in licorice-black leather add a soft sheen.

CLASSIC AMERICAN COMFORT. That's what underscores the elements in this mix. Thanks to its rounded back and sides, this midcentury-modern-style barrel chair is especially roomy for relaxing. A solid-hued pillow helps soften the look of the print, shown off to good advantage on this clean-lined shape. Dark wood feet coordinate with the other furnishings.

CHAPTER 6

Imagine Your Rooms Naked

Space-planning and furniture-arranging tips

Comfort comes not only from the right furniture but also from furniture properly placed. Here's help in figuring out what goes where. Study our floor-plan ideas for living rooms of different shapes and sizes. Then try our step-by-step method for balancing furnishings and positioning them to best suit a room's functions. **BEFORE YOU START, ANSWER THESE QUESTIONS ABOUT YOUR ROOM:** 1. *How will you use it?* Take time to visualize its functions. For the next week jot down everything you do there. For instance in a family room will you watch TV, entertain guests, or both? Will you read in a quiet corner, or can you get lost in a book anywhere? Will you eat meals or snacks in front of the TV? Will a dog be lounging in there? Do children need to study? 2. *What do you want people to see when they enter the room?* What's your favorite feature? Can you make it the focal point? Is it a great view, welcoming fireplace, or inviting conversation area with sumptuous sofa? If the room has several entry points, balance the view from each. 3. *Which other rooms connect to it?* Consider promoting tranquillity by visually linking the color scheme or decorating style of rooms that open onto one another.

Layouts for Living Rooms

Your living room may have more potential than you think. Here are some furniture arrangements to help you unlock it.

We took three popular living room shapes and created three furniture plans for each. They suit private times as well as entertaining and handle a range of activities. All have points in common. **LESS IS MORE:** Leave space to walk between furnishings. Remember how crowded a room gets with a house full of people. Design routes through rooms that don't cross conversation areas. **USE IT ALL:** Put a chaise in a corner for reading. Decorate from floor to ceiling by including tall pieces like étagères or art above low pieces. **INFORMAL BALANCE OVER SYMMETRY:** Symmetry forms mirror images, like identical tables and lamps flanking a sofa, which can be static. Informal balance is more creative—a tall piece on one side and a shorter piece displaying tall objects on the other.

The L-Shape Living Room

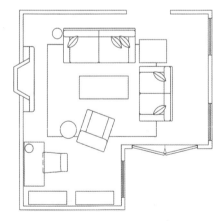

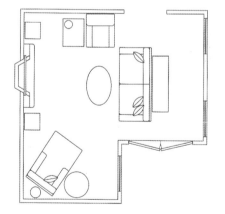
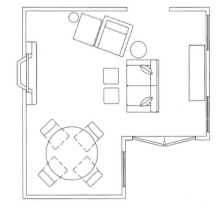

STUDY IN THE L. A rug centers the main seating area, which creates a cozy conversation grouping across from the fireplace. Behind it, a second activity spot has a desk for studying, with bookcases for storing school supplies.

READING NOOK IN THE L. A sofa faces the fireplace and flat-panel TV above it. In a quiet corner, a book lover's paradise: comfy chaise with side table for drinks and standing lamp for light. The chaise also has a backyard view.

GAME TABLE IN THE L. A club chair angles in to catch a view of the flat-panel TV over the fireplace. You also can see the TV from a seat at the table, making it an ideal spot to grab some tube time while working on a favorite hobby.

The Large Open-Plan Living Room

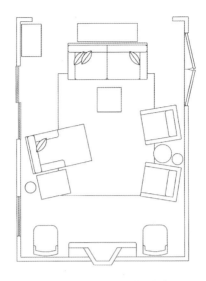

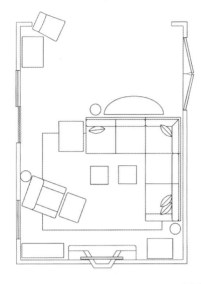

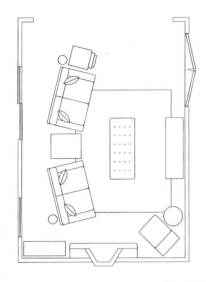

MEDIA-FREE ZONE. A lovely living room, sans TV, is appealing for entertaining. Two club chairs encourage quiet tête-à-têtes. Two smaller "pull-ups" by the fireplace can be moved where needed. A console behind the sofa is a good display space for collectibles.

FLAT SCREEN OVER FIREPLACE. Which side of the sectional you sit on will depend on whether you want to see the TV or the garden through the patio doors. The arrangement leaves clear paths from other rooms to the yard. A secretary turns a corner into a study.

ENTERTAINMENT ARMOIRE. Little kids will probably love watching TV from the bench ottoman, which they seem to think of as their own private sofa. Pets will probably join them. Note that the nesting tables serving as an end table may encourage "TV dinners."

The Small Square Living Room

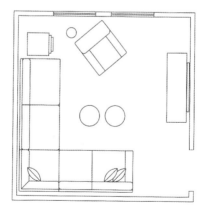

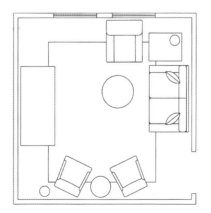

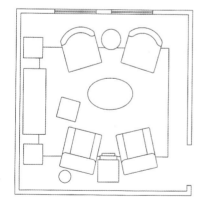

L-SHAPE SECTIONAL. Consisting of an armless love seat, corner piece, and left-arm love seat, a sectional makes this a snug setting to cocoon in. Hanging a TV over a low buffet or a console table gives you convenient media storage.

ALL YOU NEED IS A LOVE SEAT. When space is tight, let a love seat stand in for a sofa. No more than two people usually sit on a sofa anyway. If you like to stretch out, substitute a round ottoman for that round table so you can put your feet up.

FOUR CHAIRS. Everyone gets equal billing in a quartet of chairs around an oval cocktail table. The setup is especially conducive to conversing with company. Accent tables make serving snacks a breeze. Étagères and a sideboard let you display collections.

Okay, we have two guys, a bulldog, and an empty room. Now what? Think in terms of "layers"—placing upholstered pieces, then tables, storage, accessories, and flowers. With each layer keep things balanced so that the colors, sizes, and layout of the furnishings give an overall soothing effect. **THE REAL STEP 1:** Before you move anything, plan on graph paper with furniture drawn to scale. Another way to save your back and your relationships is to make full-size cardboard cutouts of furnishings and arrange them on the floor. **START WITH THE SOFA:** Its location helps determine a room's functions. Will it face a TV? Will it center a conversation area? **WATCH YOUR WEIGHT:** Furnishings have physical and visual weight. In a room full of light colors, even a small piece in a dark hue will be a focal point. Avoid sharp contrasts that disturb tranquillity. >>> Turn the page to see us create a Soft + Modern living room in this space.

How to Balance a Room

> **"** Being a Libra, I like balance. If a room is balanced, it gives me a certain calm. To create balance, I'll keep the lines of each piece of furniture parallel or perpendicular to the other pieces. Occasionally I'll throw in a different angle, but even then at least two pieces will be turned in that same direction." — *Bob*

Lulu's Step-by-Step Guide

1 Roll out the rug and **start the first layer** with the sofa. At 96 inches wide, it can comfortably accommodate three people sitting or one reclining.

2 Position the sofa so that just its front legs are on the rug. Let the rug **define a conversation area.** This rug is 8×10 feet. Pieces set around it will be cozy enough for quiet talk.

5 Bring in a coffee table that's long and low like the sofa and a side table that's square like the chairs. **You want convenience**—surfaces near all seating to set down drinks.

6 **Break up the low lines** of the room with a tall piece. This armoire has a lighter-wood inlay that ties it to the wood tables.

9 Center a photograph over the sofa. Its dark frame repeats the deep tones of the armoire, while its shape mirrors the chairs. It also forms a **balanced triangle** with the chairs.

10 Layer in accessories. Vases on the armoire **introduce roundness** and pick up colors in the photo and fabrics. The glass vase on the coffee table echoes the glass lamp base.

3 Balance the sofa with two chairs in a print whose background complements the sofa fabric. A print has more **visual weight** than a solid, which helps these smaller pieces hold their own.

4 Use two pairs of toss pillows—smaller ones in the chair print, larger ones in a rich accent color from the print—to link the sofa and chairs. **So far, so symmetrical.**

7 Something needs to go opposite the side table. It could be another side table, but **go with the unexpected** and put the armoire there instead.

8 Place a tall lamp on the side table to **balance the armoire's height.** Then lessen the focus on the armoire with a unique accent table whose dark finish stands out against the chair.

11 Bring closure—and **add more seating**—to the conversation area with two corner chairs with wood legs finished to complement the tables.

12 To **enhance design interest,** arrange the chairs in traditional tête-à-tête fashion. Then get a dog in colors to match to pose by your side (wink).

CHAPTER 7

Master the Mix

Keys to combining furniture, fabrics, and collectibles

Mixing has its advantages. You can work in pieces you already own, create a personal look, and easily update the look over time. Here are ideas for blending diverse furniture styles and creating soothing color combos to make your rooms tranquil and timeless. You'll also find suggestions for incorporating accessories and starting collections, plus tips on shopping at one of our favorite venues: the flea market.

The Unexpected Furniture Mix

Can these pieces be mixed? Yes, especially if you think of it as collecting rather than decorating. Your goal is to pick furnishings that, in five years, you'll still want to live with. Then you'll be able to update simply by changing a slipcover or rearranging a few pieces. The interesting shapes will keep rooms looking fresh. **MIX MASTERED:** We love how the mix gives everyone a chance to get a unique look without resorting to the uncomfortably artsy or trendy. But what makes pieces work together? *In this assemblage, notice that there are plenty of points of interest but no jarring notes.* Each piece has a simple, classic shape that stands out beautifully like a sculpture. Details like tufting, turning, and hardware add design interest. Many pieces have materials in common. For instance, walnut trim on the modern mirrored chest ties it to the traditional "executive assistant," whose mirrored doors reinforce the connection.

ARE THEY FLEA MARKET FINDS? They may look like it, but most of these furnishings are available in stores. You can see many of these pieces in the room arrangements in Chapter 5. Note that it's often easiest to blend furnishings in contrasting materials. For example, two medium-tone wood pieces might be hard to combine. One finish might be more yellow, the other, more red, which could be uncomfortable to the eye. A simpler solution: Pair wood with metal, mirror, or rattan.

"Collecting. To some it's a hobby. To me it's a borderline addiction … discovering pieces from yesterday that translate seamlessly into today's modern world. On its own, each piece is unique with an interesting story to tell. But together, their unified voice speaks of comfort, hospitality, warmth, and a little humor." —*Bob*

The Color and Texture Mix

> " For us, green is relaxing. We like the idea of putting it on a piece made for unwinding."
> — *Bill and Karrie, Hickory, North Carolina*

Easy on the eyes yet interesting and inviting. On these pages you'll find fabric combinations to help you achieve that effect in your rooms. The examples might inspire color schemes for your whole house, an upholstery group, or the pillows to dress up your sofa. **A LITTLE IS A LOT:** Soothing colors aren't always pale or soft. Vibrant hues have their place. Our rule of thumb is no more than three or four colors in a room, with most used as accents. Don't base color choices on trends—think about what you'd like living with long-term. Certain combinations are sure bets, such as those found in nature. You also could borrow hues from a painting, pottery, or your favorite shirt; the colors don't have to be in something that will actually end up in the room.

THE RIGHT WHITE. The print inspired the color combination, opposite. Note that those rosy hues could "pop" too much against plain white walls. To soften the contrast, we prefer white walls with some texture, whether it's painted-over brick or paneling or a subtle technique for applying paint to drywall. We also recommend a softer ivory white. Even in modern settings, it is more flattering to people, pets, and objects.

COLOR + TEXTURE INSPIRATION. A Soft + Modern color blend enlivens this clean-lined taupe sofa. You could alter its look simply by exchanging the pale blue pillows for pink or a brown stripe. That's why we're fans of solid fabrics in neutral or classic colors for main upholstery pieces. It makes them very affordable to update. Using fabrics of different textures is a sure way to generate richness. Combining leather with linen, velvet, and chenille takes the layering to the next level, as the photos opposite, top and bottom right, show.

Closeup: Coffee Tables

We like wood as much as the next guy. A cherry-veneer coffee table like the one shown at left is a beautiful thing. However, we've found a few other options that can really raise your comfort level and help blend a mix of furnishings. **THE BENCH OTTOMAN:** This long, low rectangle feels so good when you put your feet up. At parties it's extra seating. Topped with trays, it's a place to serve. **MULTIPLES:** Groups of two, three, or four cubes please the eye by breaking up an expanse of sofa. And they're flexible—rearrange as needed. **THE ROUND OTTOMAN:** Round and oval pieces bring welcome curves to straight-line settings. **TIES THAT BIND:** Fabric ottomans give rooms a softer feel and reinforce color schemes by coordinating with other fabrics. Leather ottomans add warmth. Rattan and metal pieces let you layer on more texture.

" I admire this coffee table's attitude. Simple and to the point—and the sky's the limit on what style room it can work in. If you have kids, though, you probably shouldn't show them the surfing thing." — *Matt, San Mateo, California*

SIZE WISE. Although diverse in material and style, the alternatives, opposite, suit standard coffee-table needs. A good height for a table is close to that of your sofa cushions, about 19 to 22 inches. (Another intriguing possibility does stand taller: the high tea table, usually between 24 and 30 inches.) And comfort also comes from having at least 18 inches between your sofa and table so you can maneuver around.

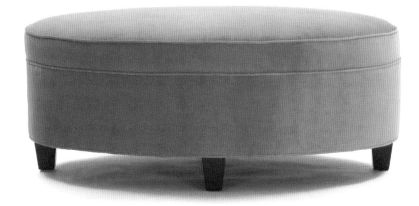

Sweet Obsessions

Here's what we mean by acquiring what you love: The pieces on the 18th-century chest, opposite, make us smile. Their free spirit, sense of humor, and bold colors really liven up a room. **OUTSIDER ART:** The angel, devil, and painting are part of this broad category, defined as work done outside the mainstream art world by self-taught artists. Often it is by artists with mental disabilities or those living lives isolated from cultural influences. You can get a sense of how diverse this field is by visiting the annual Outsider Art Fair in New York.

TRANSFER OF PASSION: Years ago our friends Reed and Paula Krosnick, a pair with great style who have been flea marketing since they began driving, sparked our interest in folk art. We had found a "memory pot," a glass jar covered in clay with little charms stuck in it, and their enthusiasm and knowledge of our find soon had us scouring flea markets for more. A few

years later, a visit to Mitchell's cousin Judy, owner of Judy A. Saslow Gallery in Chicago, forged our connection to outsider art. We spent several nights at her apartment, filled with her expansive collection. It was like sleeping in a museum. And it made us fall in love with outsider art.

> " Bob's smile says it all: There's nothing like the thrill of the hunt, whether for one-of-a-kind works of art or readily available items like snow globes." — *Mitchell*

COLLECT FOR THE FUN OF IT. Snow globes, above left, are easy and affordable to acquire, especially for people often in airports. On the chest, opposite, outsider art mixes with a tramp art "crown of thorns" cross, which is made of pointed interlocking sticks. Beside it is a papier-mâché dog, a contemporary piece with outsider roots.

Bob's Flea Market Tips

Many accessories in our homes are from flea markets. Besides stretching a budget, fostering creativity, and helping Mother Earth through reuse, flea markets are fun. Here's how to ensure enjoyable forays:

1. PLAN. At big flea markets, it's easy to get overwhelmed. If you need specific items, make a mental shopping list. For general decorating start a running list and check off items you find. Decide in advance what you're willing to pay by seeing what items cost new and what collectibles go for. Or make a budget and tabulate as you buy.

2. COLLECT. Experience the fun of the hunt by focusing on at least one affordable and plentiful item. But consider what sizes and quantity you can fit in your home. Research your favorite collectibles to learn to spot "the real thing."

3. MEASURE. Always carry dimensions of your spaces and bring a tape measure. That way if you need a table for a 38-inch wall, you won't buy a 40-inch one that looked like it would fit. Also bring measurements of display spots, such as shelf heights in a curio cabinet.

4. BRING SOME ESSENTIALS. Creature comforts help you think on your feet: water, a snack, hat, sunglasses, sunscreen, walking shoes. Other aids: a magnifying glass to read imprints on jewelry; cash in small bills; a large tote or backpack; boxes, newspaper, and bubble wrap to ensure safe transport. Some flea markets offer a shipping service, but figure in that cost before you buy.

5. GO EARLY. That easily can mean 6 a.m. A lot of the items are one-of-a-kind. It's a competitive sport.

6. TAKE TWO. Don't go with a bigger crowd than three unless you agree in advance to split up. Cell phones help you reconnect—especially for second opinions. With some cell phones, you can photograph finds and e-mail images to a partner at home for a consult—but ask dealers first.

TRAMP ART. These frames give you a feel for this amazing folk-art form. We love the intricate handiwork and how it uses ordinary materials that would have otherwise been discarded. Despite its romantic name, tramp art is believed to be mainly by early-1900s itinerant craftsmen, not hobos. They cut strips from cedar cigar boxes, edge-notched them, and glued them together. Works range from boxes to rare large furnishings.

7. DECIDE QUICKLY. An item might not be there later. What's your instinct about its worth? For collectibles, make notes of price ranges guidebooks suggest.

8. JOT IT DOWN. If you buy things you can't carry, vendors will hold them for you. But get receipts and write down booth numbers so you can find them later. Some flea markets close at a certain hour; leave time to retrieve your purchases.

9. HAGGLE—NICELY. Reed, our flea market buddy, has an easygoing method that we find usually works. Simply say, "What's your best, best, best price?" and smile. Whatever you do, don't knock the product. Shopping at day's end can mean better prices. Be prepared to walk away if something's over your budget, thanking the sellers very much. You'll be surprised to find they'll sometimes change their minds.

10. FALL IN LOVE. That's the reason to buy something. If you're trying to buy it because you think it's going to be valuable, buy stock instead.

MCCOY POTTERY. Collecting this popular American art pottery will let you score at most flea markets. Prices have risen since we started in 1982, but the pottery is still accessible. Made from the 1920s to 1990, McCoy features simple shapes in rich hues that suit modern or traditional decors. For impact, display several shapes in the same color together. And enjoy its practicality: Use finds as serving bowls, planters, or vases.

Some Places We Got Lucky

CALIFORNIA: The Rose Bowl, Pasadena; www.rosebowlstadium.com; bimonthly. Santa Monica Antiques Market; 323-933-2511; monthly.

GEORGIA: Lakewood 400 Antiques Market, Cumming; monthly; lakewoodantiques.com. Scott Antique Market, Atlanta; monthly; scottantiquemarket.com.

MASSACHUSETTS: Brimfield Antiques & Collectibles Shows, Brimfield; www.brimfieldshow.com; three times a year.

MICHIGAN: First Sunday Antiques Market, Centreville; 715-526-9769; monthly, May-August & October.

NEW YORK: Annex/Hells Kitchen Flea Market & West 25th St. Market; hellskitchenfleamarket.com; weekends

NORTH CAROLINA: Metrolina Expo Flea Market, Charlotte; 800-824-3770; monthly.

TEXAS: Round Top, near Round Top, Texas; folk art, 281-493-5501; first weekend in April & October. Canton Flea Market, Canton; 903-567-2991; monthly.

Traders Village Flea Market, Grand Prairie; 972-647-2331; weekends.

PARIS: Les Puces de Saint Ouen, between Porte de St-Ouen and Porte de Clignancourt. Marche aux Puces de la Porte de Vanves, Avenue Georges Lafenestre. Marche aux Puces de Montreuil, Avenue de la Porte de Montreuil. All three, Saturday-Monday.

Collecting Points of View

We've always loved photography. In our early days we simply bought and framed postcards. We also found old photos at flea markets. And our rooms feature lots of family photos, some lovingly handed down for generations (and a few we had to beg our parents to part with). **WHAT WILL YOU COLLECT?** Start with what appeals to you, and from there you'll find other things that speak to you in new ways. When we started collecting, we went to a New York gallery to buy black-and-white photos shot at night. However, when we got there, as is our way, we insisted on seeing everything in those cool thin-drawer file cabinets. While we grooved on the subtle moodiness of black and white, we found that oversize color photos drew us in. Today we collect color and black-and-white works by Southern photographers, an homage to our wonderful life down South. Recently we helped our friend Tipper Gore assemble the first collection of her photography. Tipper has been taking pictures since her husband, Al, gave her a camera more than 30 years ago. From her early stint at a Nashville paper through the many special moments her political life has allowed her to witness, the collection takes us along.

> **"** Great photography lets you view the world through one artist's eyes. It's totally honest, capturing not just the image but the emotion of a subject." —*Bob*

YOU NEVER KNOW WHAT YOU'LL SEE. That's what Tipper Gore has told us. The collection of photos, opposite, makes us glad she brought her camera along over the years. Grouping images together like this is a good way to tell the story of a fascinating journey through life. Note that these photos are framed with acrylic glazing material rather than glass. Framers recommend this option if photos must be shipped, if you move a lot, or if they'll hang in a high-traffic area.

KEYS TO A QUALITY FRAME. First select one that enhances art and doesn't distract from it. Respect the spirit of an image, understand where it was captured, and decide the best size to view it. Curators require that materials used to frame fine-art photos meet conservation standards, which ensure that if a photo is removed from its frame, it will be in the same condition as when it went in. Ask for conservation-grade mat and UV-filtering glass or acrylic to minimize light damage because even if art is not exposed to direct sun, UV rays still can damage it.

Final Touches: Adding Accessories and Flowers

Accessories:
There are no hard-core rules. The key is to take what you have and figure out how it works best together. For instance, do you want to arrange a bunch of vases from shortest to tallest or put the tallest in the middle? The decision, of course, is personal, but it also involves developing a good eye. Look for display ideas in books and magazines, people's homes, store presentations, and museum exhibits. Experiment by setting up items several ways; try living with each for a day if you're unsure.

AVOID CLUTTER BUT MAKE IT WARM. Use enough collectibles to make an impact but leave space for your eye to rest and shapes to be appreciated.

DECIDE WHETHER YOU WANT TO GROUP OBJECTS THAT ARE THE SAME OR DIFFERENT. Also look at textures and colors. Do you prefer a mix of materials or ones that are all the same? Perhaps you'd like an eye-catching display of different pieces in the same color.

THREE SEEMS TO BE A MAGIC NUMBER. Try using something high, low, and in the middle. And stagger the objects instead of lining them up. The three points form an "endless circle" that creates an enjoyable path for the eye.

ODD NUMBERS IN GENERAL GIVE YOU ARRANGEMENTS THAT ARE BALANCED WITHOUT BEING STAID AND SYMMETRICAL. For instance, five smaller objects could visually balance a large object.

IT DOESN'T HAVE TO COST A FORTUNE. What we particularly like about the accessories at Camp Hickory is that they look expensive but are mainly flea market finds, so we don't worry about kids or grown-ups who like to touch. For peace of mind, put valuables out of reach.

Flowers:
You usually see two main kinds of flower arrangements. There's the big front-and-center kind that becomes the focus of a room, which is what you tend to get when you order from florists without specifying what you want. (It's sort of their job.) Then there's the arrangement that becomes part of a room rather than upstaging it. Shouldn't flowers be an accessory? Here's help in keeping them simple.

"SIMPLE" DOESN'T ALWAYS MEAN SMALL. It means not having a million things stuck into an arrangement. The right size depends on where the flowers are displayed. If you're peering around flowers on a table, they're too big.

WHEN YOU'RE NOT SURE WHAT TO USE, GO WITH WHITE FLOWERS. They're easiest to work with because they complement everything.

SIMPLICITY ALSO COMES FROM ONE KIND OF FLOWER IN ONE COLOR. Try a bowl of red tulips, a vase of yellow daffodils.

FLOWERS DO NOT NEED TO BE ELABORATE OR EXPENSIVE. You can go into your yard—not even your garden—and clip bits of a shrub to arrange in a jar.

OUR PET PEEVE: FLOWERS OUT OF SEASON. That's what we don't like about fake flowers. You go into someone's house in winter and see sunflowers, which you know don't bloom then. You can get a list of seasonal flowers for your area. Or just go with what you see outside.

Beyond Furnishings: Mitchell's Top Five True Comforts

1. ALL LIGHTS ON DIMMERS. Let them help you set a relaxed mood in every room—even the bath.

2. SOFT TOWELS. This is true luxury, like you'd find in a five-star hotel. And be sure to have big body-enveloping ones for baths.

3. RADIANT-HEAT BATHROOM FLOORS. Put them on timers. Mine is set for a half hour before I wake up. It's cozy on bare feet.

4. BLACKOUT DRAPERIES OR SHADES IN BEDROOMS. Why should the sun dictate how late you sleep? Especially if you travel a great deal like we do, you need to catch up after too many late-night flights.

5. GREAT GUEST ACCOMMODATIONS. Whether it's a separate room, part-time study, or living-room sofa bed, a great guest room is about a welcoming state of mind. **NICETIES:** all-cotton sheets, extra pillows and blankets, a few good books or magazines, a small reading light, fresh flowers (but ask about allergies first), alarm clock, extra toiletries (hotel-size ones are good), tissues, water glass, suitcase stand, mirror, trash can, and extra bars or hooks in the bathroom for guests' towels.

CHAPTER 8

Three Ways To Enhance Your Love Life

An ode to slipcovers, furniture to share, and the piece of your dreams

Some furnishings bring you closer to the people (and pets!) in your life. Slipcovered sofas encourage more relaxed entertaining and family time because they're easy-care. Chair-and-a-halfs and sectionals invite playing and talking together. And having one very special piece you've fallen for—whether because it keeps you organized, reminds you of when you were young, or thrills you to look at—will warm your heart daily. Try adding these harmony and happiness helpers to your rooms.

> " Why this sofa? The comfort. And the white slipcover is classic. Plus, in truth, I don't like wearing clothes, and this sofa reminds me of when I get to go places on vacation where I don't have to."
> — Wade, San Diego

SLIPCOVERS: Relaxed

Whatever you don't want him to do on the sofa, you'll mind it less if the sofa is slipcovered. As we like to say, "Slipcovers are about living with less stress. And more life." Among the benefits: **PERFECT FOR PERFECTIONISTS.** It's hard to stay mad when he spills on a washable slipcover. Pets can nap in peace. Kids can put their feet up. Guests will feel

AN IMPORTANT LESSON. We like slipcovers because they look relaxed, are easy-care, and let you change with the seasons. Note, however, that there are slipcovers called "one-size-fits-all." Frankly we don't like them and suggest you avoid them. They look messy and cheap (sorry, but we can't think of a more polite word). We've found that the best way to manufacture a slipcovered piece is to make a "muslin base"—a sofa or chair, say, upholstered in a thin cotton—and then sew a slipcover to fit that particular base precisely. This will give you the relaxed but well-tailored look you're after.

and Ready for Action

more at ease. And you can stress less with a second slipcover for emergencies. **COOL WITH COMMITMENT-PHOBES.** Not sure white denim will always be the one? Slipcovers keep your options open. **SUPERB FOR SEASONAL MOOD SWINGERS.** Sometime after Labor Day you may feel the desire to exchange white denim for green velvet or crème chenille.

LOOK 1. The sofa is welcoming in its rich butter slipcover, which fits casually yet neatly, like clothes for Sunday brunch. Underneath, the sofa is upholstered in muslin, which creates a smooth surface so the slipcover lies flat. Pillows link the sofa and wing chair.

One Sofa, Two Looks

Change rocks. Sometimes you just feel like making a new style statement.

LOOK 2. Now see the sofa in an awning stripe, a fun mix with the ticking stripe on the chair. We've found that a simple change of slipcover from solid to pattern like this causes people to say, "Oh, you redecorated the room." Just the effect we were hoping for.

With slipcovers it's easy. >>> For more reasons to change, turn the page.

One Room, Two Seasons

Transforming this living room from first buds to last leaves meant changing only slipcovers, pillows, flowers, and a few accessories.

SPRING INTO SUMMER: For a fresh look that takes you right through summer in style, try dressing your upholstery in a light-color cotton ticking stripe. Khaki on the ottoman is a nice bridge between the seating and darker rattan tables. **CONSIDER OTHER OPTIONS:** Slipcovers in crisp white denim or chalky-blue linen would have an equally invigorating effect.

COMPARE + CONTRAST. Choose slipcovers in the same fabric for your sofa and chair, as shown here, for a unifying effect. Or select slipcovers in two different fabrics, as shown opposite, to expand the seasonal color palette of your room.

COMFORT FACTORS. As the Victorians knew, outfitting furniture in light-color, lightweight slipcovers helps the whole room feel cooler. The bench ottoman wears another warm-weather favorite, prewashed khaki, which has the added benefit of a wonderfully soft hand.

FALL INTO WINTER: Changing slipcover material as well as color makes this cold-day conversion a tactile and visual pleasure. Red chenille on the sofa, gold chenille on the chair, and chocolate velvet on the ottoman feel warm and look rich. **START A TRADITION:** Signal summer's end and reestablish the back-to-school mood with a slipcover switch-out. Or at holiday time make your decorating even more memorable with seasonally appropriate slipcovers that truly transform a room.

PILLOW POWER. The right pillows can do so much. This striped one contains all the colors in the setting, enhancing the room's pulled-together look. The relaxed yet tailored style of the slipcovers also contributes; rather than "one-size-fits-all," they're designed for their pieces.

BEST FOR GUESTS. Slipcovers help guests feel more relaxed because they don't need to worry as much about spills. And then there's the ultimate insurance: a second set for emergencies. Red and brown are particularly practical choices for party people because the dark colors don't show stains or wear.

Two Chairs, Four Styles

Upholstered dining chairs truly are wonderful. They look and feel soft and really can change the personality of a room. Add to those benefits the transformative power of slipcovers, as illustrated at left. The side chair goes from warm wintry charm to romantic summer sophistication with a short slipcover that shows off its turned legs. The armchair offers two versions of casual modern style: a ticking stripe with tapered legs and a relaxed-fit, floor-grazing slipcover. **COMFORT FACTORS:** Before buying chairs, measure your table. Most are about 30 inches high, so a chair's seat height should be about 19 to 20 inches, giving your legs at least 10 inches between the chair and the tabletop or apron. To decide how many chairs can fit around a table, allow at least 24 inches per person. For a rectangular table, add 12 inches at each end for diners at the head and foot. Position your table about 36 inches from walls or furniture so people can pull out chairs easily.

SLIPCOVERED WITH STYLE. A dress Gwyneth Paltrow wore to the Oscars inspired the chairs, opposite. They are easy-care like their slipcovered sisters because they wear low-maintenance faux suede. We manufacture the slipcovers on the chairs, above left, to fit them perfectly, which gives a cleaner silhouette than one-size-fits-all options. The chairs can wear versatile white, but you also can experiment with color, perhaps using two complementary hues around a table. Also consider upholstered chairs at the ends of a table and slipcovered chairs on the sides.

> "Sure, I'm really comfortable reading at the table, but come on, don't you think these chairs are just meant for a nice long romantic dinner for two?"
> *—Justin, Hickory, North Carolina*

1

What you sit in can change how you relate. **1. CONVERSATION CHAIRS:** We once attended a conference where speakers sat in armchairs instead of standing at podiums. Their talks so surpassed typical seminar fare that we couldn't help thinking that the comfy chairs had an effect. This also could work at home. **2. CHAIR AND A HALF:** With a matching ottoman it's like a double chaise, just easier to get out of. It's also a great parent-

Ways to Stay Connected

2

3

4

5

and-child reading chair, sure to inspire a wonderful habit. **3. ONE-ARM CHAISES:** Put a left- and right-arm together. Or use them individually if your decorating needs change. **4. CORNER CHAIRS:** Similarly flexible, they can be a love seat or sit separately. **5. DAYBED:** Besides the snuggle potential, this one has a twin-bed-size cushion that can sleep an overnight guest.

> **❝** You can live in this: read, sleep, eat, work, watch TV. And there's room for a close friend. You just need to get out once in a while to wash the slipcover."
> —*George, Hickory, North Carolina*

Sectionals Are for Sharing Too

Here's another way to get closer: sectionals. Inviting and sociable-looking, they suit media rooms, family rooms, and living rooms. A small one even might fit in a master suite. Sectionals also offer flexibility. They're usually sold as components, which lets you choose the right size pieces for your room. Some components work equally well as stand-alones, so you can create a larger conversation area by facing one with, say, armless chairs or a love seat. You'll also appreciate a sectional made of smaller components on moving day: It breaks down to go in and out of a room more easily.

SHOES OFF. With chalky-blue cotton slipcovers and beach-ball pillows, the modular sectional, right, has the feel of a swimming pool. Note that the two front ottomans are lower, creating a stepped effect. Bob designed a mini version of the big sectional, above left, using a love seat, a corner, and an ottoman as an easy-care command center for one. The ottoman can be moved aside when you're ready to get out.

OPTIONS ABOUND. Reminiscent of "love pits" from the 1970s, the 11-piece arrangement, right, includes corner pieces, armless love seats, and armless chairs. It's easy to envision its hosting a slumber party. The U-shape setup, above right, with two cubes for a coffee table, is a good everyday alternative if you prefer not to climb in. An L-shape armless sectional, above, faces a matching love seat. With four cubes as additional seating, the group can handle big gatherings. And here's what memories are made of, opposite: Can't you just picture her all grown up, telling people about the great beach-ball pillows her family had when she was little?

> **“** **I love this stuff. It's the ultimate media room furniture.”**
> — *What we think Maddy, age 5, Hickory, North Carolina, was thinking when this was taken*

THE PIECE OF YOUR DREAMS
Everybody Needs One. What's Yours?

There are things you shouldn't have to explain—your attraction to someone, or something, being one of them. The fun and friendly team members at Mitchell Gold + Bob Williams, however, were glad to share what moves them. Eight of them tell all here. The rest dish throughout the book. Let them inspire you to get a special piece of your own.

" What do I like about this chair? Color is number one. Then shape. And also the way it sits—such great support for my back. The chair has so much character. I could imagine decorating a whole room around it."
— *Jason, Dallas*

" Elegant pieces are usually so traditional. This one has more modern elegance. Its clean lines could work in many rooms of my home. But I'd definitely put it in my bedroom."
— *Robin, Hickory, North Carolina*

" I want a home comfortably furnished so that it's calm and relaxing visually, physically, and mentally. But I also love uniqueness, those special pieces in a room that captivate. This table is like a sculpture with soft, comfortable lines."
— *Rip, Chicago*

> " To me, things in a home are visuals of who we are. In my case, this lamp says it all: simple yet dramatic, elegant but doesn't take herself too seriously. A little Audrey Hepburn. A little Bette Midler. It makes me smile."
> — *Victoria, Santa Monica*

> " I'm a little bit country and a little bit rock 'n' roll. This chair is traditional yet hip. A perfect Sunday would be me in it, reading the paper or catching up with friends by phone."
> — *Ryan, Washington, D.C.*

> " I love the mix of light and dark woods. When you live in Manhattan, it's nice to have something that captures the light. The beautiful blond interior seems to glow. And it highlights anything I display against it." — *Sean, New York*

> " This sofa is simply elegant and elegantly simple. I'd like my life to be this simple and elegant. I love the way the sofa curves. It's also deceptively comfortable. And it has a real midcentury feel, my favorite period, stylewise." — *Richard, Kendall Park, New Jersey*

> " I love the shape of this wing chair. It's a classic redefined to fit even modern rooms. And the unexpected fabric is like pairing a suit jacket with jeans—tradition with a twist. As for Henry, he mainly sees it as another place to jump up and be admired from all angles."
> — *Robert with Henry, New York*

CHAPTER 9

Shop Talk

How to make the trip easier

It's amazing to see all the handcrafting that goes into fine furniture. To give you a sense of it and an idea of what's inside a piece of upholstery, we're about to take you to our factory floor and show step-by-step the birth of a leather chair. You'll also get help making the whole furniture-buying experience more relaxing, learning how to measure properly, what to bring to the store, and how to stop agonizing over which sofa to buy.

Where Do Chairs Come From?

We'll never lose our fascination with the factory floor. The handwork that goes into each piece is amazing to watch. Here's a behind-the-scenes look at the highlights of creating an MG+BW icon, the Parisian leather club chair. This style chair is a good example of our design synergy. We first saw the chairs while browsing at a Paris flea market, and we knew immediately not only that we had to make them but also that we had to enhance their comfort by upgrading their scale to American size. **NOTE:** A few of the steps shown opposite happen concurrently. For instance, while the frame is built and "sprung up," the cover is cut and sewn. This allows a finished frame and cover to arrive at the bench of the craftsperson upholstering the chair at the same time.

UNOFFICIAL CHAIR TESTERS. Jace, Carter, Akina, and Lauren from our day-care center deem the product their parents help create strong and durable. (We, of course, only encourage chair climbing in photos.) A special shout-out goes to the many other members of our team who helped in making this chair, from materials purchasers to production schedulers to day-care teachers who take such good care of our kids.

STEP 1. Designs are hand-drawn then patterns made by computer.

STEP 2. Kiln-dried hardwood frame parts are cut and arranged for assembly.

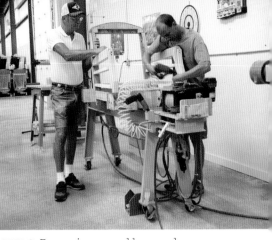

STEP 3. Frame is secured by wood dowels, glued, and high-pressure nailed.

STEP 4. Steel springs are attached to back and seat then covered in batting.

STEP 5. Meanwhile, the chair pattern is marked on leather hides and cut out.

STEP 6. A sewer stitches the leather pieces into a complete chair cover.

STEP 7. At the upholsterer's bench, the frame is padded and cover attached.

STEP 8. Nailhead trim is applied by hand, skillfully aligned by eye.

STEP 9. After multiple inspections the chair is wrapped and boxed for transport.

Fun with Furniture:
How to Relax and Buy It

Before you shop. Knowing what you like will lower your stress, and we hope this book has gotten you to that point. Having the information you need to make decisions will take you the rest of the way. **STUDY:** Gathering visuals isn't just for designers. It helps you communicate with salespeople. Bob has a simple system for keeping track of things he clips from magazines: Baskets perfectly sized for magazine pages sit on his coffee table. They're portable, and the process doesn't require a lot of filing. **ANALYZE:** As hard as it may be, weed out things that aren't working. Ask a friend with style to help. Look in your rooms to see if an item you're using somewhere else might work better in the room you're decorating. For instance, a bedroom chest could be good for a living room. **MEASURE:** Don't fall for a piece that's too big for your room—or your front door. Measure doorways, stairways, and halls. For apartments, check elevators. It's a good idea to sketch your room and the route a piece will travel to get there, noting all measurements. **CARRY:** Always be prepared to buy. Don't leave home without your measurements, tape measure, pictures, paint or fabric swatches, and a notebook to jot down prices, dimensions, and salespeople's names. Bringing snapshots of your rooms also helps.

At the store. Shop at stores with a style sense like yours—just as you probably already do for clothing. **ASK:** Find a knowledgeable salesperson who is genuinely interested in your questions. Build a relationship with someone who can help with your decorating needs over time. **TELL** him or her where a piece will go, how you'll use it, styles of other pieces, and whether you have kids or pets. Rather than say what you'll pay for one item, consider an overall budget. We're proponents of "high-low" furnishing, like "high-low" dressing—a Gap T with Seven Jeans and a Prada bag. A good salesperson can help you allocate resources. **DO:** Check on comfort. If you're buying a chair, pull up the ottoman. With a sofa, don't just sit, lie down as you would at home. **GET** info sheets, digital photos, and fabric cuttings. Review them at home in the room you're considering the furniture for.

A sofa isn't destiny. People often agonize too much. Find a shape and style you like that fit your space and be sure the sofa is comfortable. **SHAPE:** In Chapter 5, you saw a range of styles and how they can mix. A skirted sofa can pair with an unskirted chair, a roll arm with a straight arm. Especially if you're starting with the sofa, pick a favorite, keep its cover simple, and be sure it meets your needs. The rest will follow. **SIZE:** Decide where a sofa will go, then measure the space carefully. Sofas are measured from outside edge of arms for width, front edge to outside of back for depth, and floor to tallest point of "hard" back (not cushions, which can be removed) for height. Three big comfort factors are seat depth, back height, and back pitch. **CUSHIONS:** Most importantly, like the "sit." Then decide how much you want to fluff. Lowest maintenance is a foam cushion wrapped in polyfiber to round the edges. Ask whether the core has a downproof casing, which replicates the pleasing "whoosh" you get when you sit on a down cushion. Next is down blend, a foam core surrounded by feathers and down in a downproof casing. Another is spring down, with coils in its foam core. Highest maintenance is, of course, all down. **COVER:** Besides color, look for durability, cleanability, and softness. A lot depends on how you live. Children or pets? Dirt-hiding dark chenille might be right. Like change? Consider a slipcover. With fine-quality leather, will you be comfortable with shading variations? Distressed leather is like antiqued wood: No two pieces are alike. **INSIDES:** Because you can't see "under the hood," ask for a spec sheet. *Frames:* Get hardwood, like maple, or state-of-the-art engineered hardwood, kiln-dried to remove moisture and prevent warping. Corner blocks screwed in place and parts doweled, glued, and high-pressure-nailed give stability. *Springs:* We developed a system of S-shape steel springs, which are closely spaced for support. Other types include eight-way hand-tied, where springs connect to adjoining ones by ties, but be aware that ties may come undone and need repairing in years to come. *Padding:* You want thick layers so you never feel the wood. We put extra padding on arms, which are often used as headrests, and on inside corners, where people snuggle. **SLEEPERS:** Yes, sleeper seats are often firmer, but the right cushions help. Get a sleeper with a recessed bar so you don't feel metal in your back when you're sleeping. We like a tilt-up headrest for TV watching and a Velcro "trapdoor" in the deck of a slipcovered sleeper so you don't have to remove the slipcover to take out the bed. **STOCK VERSUS SPECIAL ORDER:** Want your sofa right away? And want to see exactly what it looks like before you buy? Ask salespeople which are in stock. This means the exact sofa in the exact fabric is available for quick delivery. We think buying this way is best. If, however, you need a certain color or size that isn't in stock, ask about special ordering, choosing fabric and sometimes size from swatches and photos. You might have to wait from six to 26 weeks for your order.

Speak like a native. For a comprehensive "furniture-to-English" dictionary, see the Mitchell Gold + Bob Williams website, www.mgandbw.com.

The Comfort of Our Company

Our mission is simple: to make the world a more comfortable place—and not just through furniture. It starts at our home away from home, the 600,000-square-foot factory, in Taylorsville, North Carolina, that we share with more than 700 members of the Mitchell Gold + Bob Williams family. And it extends to our local and national communities through our charitable giving and ways of doing business. Here's what we stand—and sit—for. **DAY CARE:** To us, top-quality day care is a real family value. Our AAAA-rated not-for-profit Lulu's Child Enrichment Center provides an education-based curriculum for more than 70 children of our employees and community. It's great for them—and for us. Having a day-care center helps us attract an exceptional workforce, the heart of our business success. Our goal is to inspire other companies to do the same. **HIGHER EDUCATION:** Each year the day we award college scholarships to children of our employees is truly a favorite. When you live in a rural community and no one in your family has ever gone to college, higher education may not be something you've considered. This program puts the idea in families' minds, makes it viable financially, and opens up a whole new future for

comfort is coming.

inside: mattresses & microwaves

for victims of Hurricane Katrina.

donated by:

MCC
www.mccchurch.org
866.hopemcc

Mitchell Gold
+Bob Williams
www.mgandbw.com
789.5401

children. **HEALTH:** Fried fast food just wasn't working for us or our employees. So we hired a professionally trained chef and created Café Lulu, a gourmet cafeteria with a health-conscious menu. We also set up Spot's Gym, a free fitness center—which, as Dan Gauthreaux, our vice president of human resources, says, "has taken away my excuse not to exercise." In addition, we hold an annual health fair where employees can get a basic physical plus preventative screenings like mammograms—something that has led to lifesaving early detection for several individuals. **EQUALITY:** A big part of being comfortable is being accepted for who you are. We think Lulu, our English bulldog mascot, has it right: She's nice to anyone who's nice to her—regardless of race, age, gender, or sexual orientation (she doesn't even notice). We support nonprofits that promote equal rights for all people. **THE ENVIRONMENT:** It's our privilege and our responsibility to create products in a manner simpatico with preserving our precious planet. Our agenda of environmental responsibility includes using woods from resources dedicated to sustainable forest management, ozone-friendly foam cushions, and 100-percent-recyclable cartons.

Mitchell Gold
+Bob Williams

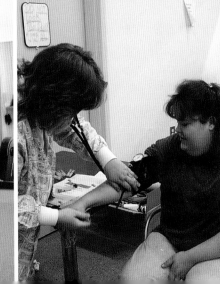

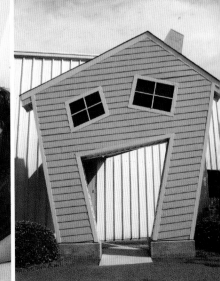

INDEX

ACKNOWLEDGMENTS

Before we wrote this book, we didn't pay much attention to Acknowledgments sections. But now, knowing all that goes into it, we definitely will—and we hope you'll read these. Our thanks to:

Mindy Drucker, who, as family member (sister-in-law) and company member, has had an insider's view of our brand of comfort. In helping us share our style, she captured the cadence, nuances, and humor of the way we talk.

Doug Turshen, art director, for his beautiful design, editorial insights, and well-seasoned advice on publishing. James Shearron, photo stylist, for his wonderful eye. Graphic designers David Huang and Steve Turner, who were great to work with.

Sally Fanjoy + James Labrenz, our photographers since the early days and also great friends.

The staff of Meredith Books, especially our open-minded and creative editor, Vicki Ingham, who was always there for us; art director Matt Strelecki; editorial director Linda Cunningham, and designer Ken Carlson.

Janis Donnaud, our agent, who "got" us even before we walked in her door, and whose enthusiasm, experience, and tell-it-like-it-is attitude fit right into our world.

The incredible MG + BW team: Charley Holt, marketer extraordinaire, with the eye for what truly expresses our brand; Eloise Goldman, who knew this was something we had to do and who helped make our project a success; Roger Turnbow, so generous with his time and talents, a proverbial fountain of ideas who advises in the nicest way; Leslie Stoll, that rare combo of creative person and master of details; Paula Krosnick, who sure knows her way around a factory and can get furniture made so fast you'd think elves did it; Richie Nelson, who helped us get things done right with a smile; and many others, among them: Justin Alberto, Victoria Amato, Nathan Banks, Laura Chapman, Joey Jagod, Reed Krosnick, Matt Langford, Bill Lattimore, Ryan Levy, Carl Marmion, Wei Shao, and Shay Starnes. Also to those who helped with the day-to-day while we stepped out into publishing, including George Ackerman, Dan Gauthreaux, John Bounous, Kevin Bowman, and Dan Swift.

The many magazine and newspaper editors who believed in us and appreciated our style. But we have to pay special tribute to Dorothy Kalins, Joe Ruggiero, Gale Steves, and Charlyne Varkonyi Schaub, who shared us with their readers very early on.

Our fantastic customers, owners of the premiere home-furnishings stores across the country, for creating such beautiful environments and featuring our products in them. The opportunity to be associated with your smarts and style is a dream come true.

The kids of Lulu's Child Enrichment Center, who teach us about comfort every day.

Our wonderful families, including Stephen Heavner, who really knows how to share, support, and stand by the people he loves, and niece Adrianne, for loaning her mom and listening to lots of business talk (it'll come in handy someday, girl).

Gay teenagers everywhere facing discrimination simply for being who you are: Be strong. You are wonderful, and you are loved. You WILL find the comfort you truly deserve.

And, our Lulu, without whose photogenic face, this book wouldn't be half as pretty.

PHOTO CREDITS

Cover + Title Page photos: Sally Fanjoy + James Labrenz

Author photo: Mindy Drucker photo by Jeff Tisman

Table of Contents: Page 6, row 3, left, and p. 7, row 1, middle, James Merrell, courtesy of *Country Home*. Page 7, row 2, middle, Mark Lund, courtesy of *Child*. Page 7, row 3, middle, Bruce Wolf, courtesy of *Child*. All others: Sally Fanjoy + James Labrenz

Intro: Lulu's baby picture, Sally Fanjoy + James Labrenz

Part One Intro: Page 10, Bruce Wolf, courtesy of *Child*

Chapter 1: James Merrell, courtesy of *Country Home*

Chapter 2: All photos except pp. 34–35 by Joshua McHugh, courtesy of *Metropolitan Home* magazine. Pages 34–35, Sally Fanjoy + James Labrenz

Chapter 3: Pages 50–53, Timothy Bell, courtesy of *House Beautiful*. Pages 54–57, King Au/Studio Au, courtesy of *Country Home*. Pages 58–59, Rick Lew, previously published in *Modern Bride*. Pages 60–61, Laura Moss, courtesy of *Country Home*. Pages 62–63, Sally Fanjoy + James Labrenz. Pages 64–65, Derek Szabo Photography. Pages 66–67, John Lei, © John Lei, 2006. Pages 68–69, Mark Lund, courtesy of *Child*. Pages 70–71, Colleen Duffley and Erica George Dines, courtesy of *Better Homes & Gardens*. Pages 72–73, Sally Fanjoy + James Labrenz

Part Two Intro: Page 74, Sally Fanjoy + James Labrenz

Chapters 4 through 9: All photos, Sally Fanjoy + James Labrenz, except: Chapter 7, p. 177, top left, and Chapter 8, pp. 199–201, by Bruce Wolf. Chapter 7, pp. 178–179, by James Merrell. Chapter 9, pp. 210–211, by MG+BW staff.

FLOOR PLANS: Laura Chapman, MG+BW

THANKS FOR SHARING

ABC Carpet & Home, New York: To Paulette Cole and Erin Johnson, PR, for loaning us some of ABC's many special items for the settings in Chapter 5.

Madeline Weinrib Atelier, ABC Carpet & Home, 6th floor: To Madeline Weinrib for lending the rugs that warm the room in Chapter 4, pp. 78, 80-93, 99.

Robert Abbey Lamps, Hickory, NC: To Jeff and Darlene Rose and Ken Wilkinson for lending the floor lamps on pp. 87-90.

Umrao Cashmere, New York: To Gurvesh Singh for loaning his company's beautiful throws, which appear in Chapter 5.